Teaching Study Skills to Students with Learning Problems

A Teacher's Guide for Meeting Diverse Needs

SECOND EDITION

John J. Hoover

James R. Patton

An International Publisher

8700 Shoal Creek Boulevard
Austin, Texas 78757-6897
800/897-3202   Fax 800/397-7633
www.proedinc.com

© 2007 by PRO-ED, Inc.
8700 Shoal Creek Boulevard
Austin, Texas 78757-6897
800/897-3202   Fax 800/397-7633
www.proedinc.com

ISBN-13: 978-141640213-8
ISBN-10: 1-4164-0213-6

Art Director: Jason Crosier
Designer: Nancy McKinney
This book is designed in FairfieldLH and Agenda.

Printed in the United States of America

1 2 3 4 5 6 7 8 9 10   10 09 08 07 06

Contents

Preface • **v**

Acknowledgments • **vii**

CHAPTER 1
Study Skills To Meet Special and Diverse Needs • **1**

What Are Study Skills? • 2
Study Skills and Learning Components • 3
Current Issues and Study Skills • 6
Study Skills and Students with Learning Problems • 15
Need for Developing Study Skills • 15
Understanding Study Skills Programs in School • 16

CHAPTER 2
Study Skills and Standards-Based Education • **17**

Standards-Based Education and Meeting Special Needs • 18
Aligning Study Skills Development with Standards • 20
Study Skills Teaching Competence • 21

CHAPTER 3
Study Skills and Lifelong Learning • **25**

Early Development of Study Skills • 27
Lifelong Importance of Study Skills • 27
Transitioning to Life Careers • 31
Life Skills, Study Skills, and Learning Components • 31

CHAPTER 4
Classroom Assessment and Implementation of Study Skills • **33**

Informal Assessment of Study Skills • 34
Planning To Meet Diverse Learning Needs • 35
Implementing a Study Skills Program • 36
Teaching Study Skills Through Cooperative Learning • 41
Semantic Webbing and Study Skills • 44

CHAPTER 5
Teaching Study Skills • **57**

Reading Rate: Key to Reading Success • 58
Listening: Comprehending Verbal Communication • 64
Graphic Aids: Understanding Visual Material • 68
Library Usage: Easy Access to Information • 73
Reference Materials: Using the Right Sources • 77
Test Taking: Improving Test Performance • 83
Notetaking and Outlining: Capturing the Main Points • 95
Report Writing: Creating Better Written Reports • 101
Oral Presentations: Building Confidence • 106
Time Management: Making Good Use of Time • 111
Self-Management: Managing Own Behaviors • 119
Organization: Managing Learning-Related Activities • 122

CHAPTER 6

**Structured Study and Learning Strategies:
A Potpourri of Formalized Techniques • 129**

Learning Strategies • 130
Study Strategies • 131

CHAPTER 7

Collaborative Model for Study Skills Programs • 143

Establishing a Collaborative Study Skills Program • 144
Collaborative Skills for Effective Change • 147

CHAPTER 8

Home-Based Study Skills Programs • 155

Home-Based Support • 156
Parental Support in Developing Study Skills • 157
Recommendations for Specific Skills Areas • 158

References • 167

About the Authors • 171

Preface

The topic of effective study habits has seen increased emphasis in the education of students, particularly those with varying degrees of learning problems. Today's students in both special and inclusive education settings are expected not only to complete assigned work but also to perform tasks in an attempt to meet ever-increasing minimum benchmark standards. The impact of the No Child Left Behind Act of 2001, the Individuals with Disabilities Education Improvement Act of 2004, and three-tier instruction and standards-based education on students with learning problems is far-reaching in today's classrooms, requiring them to regularly use a variety of study and learning strategies. In addition, educators realize that students who use study skills effectively perform better in school and in lifelong learning endeavors. Unacceptably high numbers of students in U.S. schools experience learning and behavior problems or otherwise do not achieve their potentials. The inability to use study skills in school's many demanding situations contributes to the learning problems that students experience. Study skills are essential in the overall learning process, whether at the elementary, secondary, or postsecondary level.

The second edition, *Teaching Study Skills to Students with Learning Problems: A Teacher's Guide for Meeting Diverse Needs,* includes four new chapters, as well as expanded coverage of content, strategies, and processes for effectively teaching study skills. This edition includes coverage of the most current topics in education—that is, three-tier instruction, standards-based education, Response to Intervention, differentiated instruction, collaboration, and technology in the schools—and their relevance to study skills education. This revised and updated book contains eight chapters that provide educators with practical ideas, suggestions, and reproducible forms related to the development and use of study skills at school and at home. This timely book emphasizes the use of study skills within the context of actual classroom tasks rather than as isolated skills.

Chapter 1 provides an overview of study skills for students with learning problems, the importance of these study skills in learning, and their relevance to life-long skills development. It also emphasizes the significance of using study skills with students who have learning problems when differentiating instruction, in determining response to intervention, and within three-tier instruction. A section specific to meeting the study skills needs of English language learners with special needs is also included. Chapter 2 provides an overview of standards-based education, emphasizing how study skills are essential for success in meeting and assessing educational standards to meet diverse needs. Chapter 3 addresses the topics of a continuum across the grades of a study skills program, transitioning to life careers, and the interrelatedness between study skills development and lifelong learning.

Chapter 4 discusses the assessment and implementation of student uses of study skills, including general study skills program characteristics and learning components. The chapter also covers the informal assessment of student uses of study skills in the classroom, sample standards-based Individualized Education Program (IEP) study skills goals, guidelines for implementing and assessing a study skills program in the classroom, and the use of cooperative learning and semantic webbing in a study skills program. Chapter 5 presents detailed descriptions and applications of 12 study skills essential for optimal learning. This chapter discusses the importance of the use of each study skill and introduces various guides, rubrics, and checklists for teachers and students to use to facilitate an effective and ongoing study skills program in the elementary and secondary grades. Also, numerous teaching suggestions are provided for each of the 12 study skills to help students with learning problems complete learning tasks more effectively and efficiently. Chapter 6 contains a description of structured student study strategies and six learning strategies for direct use in the classroom. Each strategy is defined and outlined for easy use by teachers and students.

Chapter 7 discusses collaboration among educators to implement a successful study skills program in inclusive and special education settings. A collaborative model is presented, along with strategies and factors important to consider in an effort to create positive change associated with improving study skills education for students with learning problems. Chapter 8, which addresses home-based support for study skills development and use, emphasizes the importance of parental assistance in complementing the school study skills program and in assisting the students to develop lifelong skills. This section includes a home inventory to assist parents in identifying students' study skills needs. To bridge study skills education from the school to the home, Chapter 8 also includes numerous strategies for helping students with learning problems use study skills at home.

This practical study skills book contains many reproducible forms for assessing and implementing a comprehensive study skills program at school and home. It also includes approximately 200 study skills teaching practices, over 30 student strategies, and nearly 100 suggestions for parents to help their children with study skills at home, as well as suggested standards-based IEP goals and objectives for teaching students with learning problems to use study skills.

This book was written for special and inclusive educators who wish to develop or continue emphasizing an ongoing and integrated study skills program in Grades K through 12. The information presented here, including the guides, rubrics, and checklists, is appropriate for use in learning any content and for students with learning problems in elementary and secondary special and inclusive education settings. The contents are also appropriate for helping difficult-to-teach students acquire lifelong skills associated with study skills development as they pursue more effective and efficient ways to learn. The various guides for identifying study skills needs will assist educators, students, and parents in the overall assessment of student abilities. To maintain students' ongoing and effective study skills use, the information in this book should be applied on a regular basis within actual classroom and assessment situations. We hope that special and inclusive educators, as well as others concerned with the education of students with learning problems, will find this resource a valuable asset as they strive to improve student success in learning by building and maintaining the critical foundation of a strong study skills base in education and lifelong learning.

JJH
JRP

Acknowledgments

The publication of a book like this one would not happen without the direct and indirect assistance of many different people. When one writes an acknowledgments section of a book, a very great possibility exists that key people who made a difference will be overlooked. To anyone who falls in this group and actually reads this section to realize that we missed mentioning their name, we apologize.

We are grateful to those professionals who share an interest in this topic and whose work has influenced us. We also wish to acknowledge the countless number of teachers who have used this book over the past 20 years to help students with special needs develop and use study skills. We specifically want to thank Holly Jeffrey of Lynchburg College for helping us to identify additional student study strategies for inclusion in the study strategies table. We are also grateful to those individuals at PRO-ED who have supported us over the years and encouraged us to create this new edition, and without whom, this book would not get into print. We specifically want to thank Kathy Synatschk and Chris Anne Worsham in the books and materials department and Courtney King in the production department.

JJH
JRP

1

Study Skills To Meet Special and Diverse Needs

The development, usage, and application of study skills and study strategies are central to the effective differentiation of instruction in special and inclusive classrooms.

This chapter familiarizes teachers with the various study skills essential for learning, as well as the need for developing them and their significance in school. The chapter also discusses study skills with regard to students with learning problems, presenting several study skills program characteristics important in the overall development of such skills throughout school. The chapter provides an overview of study skills and discusses several current national educational initiatives that have a direct impact on the importance of study skills and learning strategies in the classroom. These include, among others, the No Child Left Behind Act of 2001 (NCLB), the Individuals with Disabilities Education Improvement Act of 2004 (IDEA), inclusion, differentiated instruction, Response to Instruction to determine appropriate special education services, and meeting diverse needs of English language learners (ELLs) in the classroom. This is followed by discussion of how these initiatives relate to current teaching and learning for all students in Grades K through 12.

What Are Study Skills?

As students progress through school, they continually face situations in which the ways they address problems relate directly to how successful they are in finding solutions. Students must make numerous decisions each day as they confront learning tasks in any subject area. Specific skills that students employ to acquire, record, remember, and use information efficiently provide the foundation for successful learning. As a result, students must have at their disposal a variety of tools to learn and retain information. These tools, known as study skills, help students deal with various situations in school, such as approaching a learning task, managing time, interpreting visual material, or taking a test. These study skills also help students to meet scheduled deadlines, locate information, use library and other resource people, organize assignments, and take notes. In addition, these academic support skills help students to listen effectively to lectures, write reports, give oral presentations, use library materials, study for different types of tests, and read for different purposes.

These important tasks require the use of one or more study skills on a regular basis throughout the school day. Success with schooling depends on how well students complete these as well as similar tasks, and it can be achieved best through proficient use of the following 12 specific study skills and a variety of other structured study strategies:

1. Reading rate
2. Listening
3. Graphic aids
4. Library usage
5. Reference material usage
6. Test taking
7. Notetaking and outlining
8. Report writing
9. Oral presentations
10. Time management
11. Self-management
12. Organization

In addition to some of the general in-school and out-of-school needs for developing study skills, the significance of study skills can be seen in the many specific activities students are expected to complete throughout their school years.

Comprehension of why particular study skills are significant to everyday learning assists in understanding their different uses and the potential problems that learners may experience in school. Table 1.1 illustrates the significance of each study skill in learning. Generally, the study skills can immediately benefit a variety of listening, speaking, reading, and writing activities.

Successful learning in school results in part from students' ability to understand why using study skills is necessary. One important contribution that teachers can make as they assist students with study skills development is to help them understand *why* it is important to apply these 12 study skills and *how* each will help them to succeed in school and later in life.

Each of these 12 study skills must be developed as students progress through school. (Specific definitions and elements associated with each of these skills appear in Chapter 5.) Although use of these skills may become more important when students engage in independent seatwork or in less teacher-directed activities, their effective use must prevail throughout education to ensure the best chance for success.

Study Skills and Learning Components

Study skills include competencies associated with acquiring, recording, organizing, synthesizing, remembering, and using information to learn (Hoover, 2004b). Figure 1.1 illustrates seven learning components identified from the literature that are affected by the use of study skills: acquisition, recording, location, organization,

Table 1.1
Study Skills: Tools for Learning

Study Skill	Significance for Learning
Reading rate	Reading rates vary with type and length of reading assignments.
Listening	Listening skills are necessary to complete most education tasks or requirements.
Graphic aids	Graphic aids may visually depict complex or cumbersome material in a meaningful format.
Library usage	Library usage skills facilitate easy access to much information.
Reference material usage	Independent learning may be greatly improved through effective use of reference materials and dictionaries.
Test taking	Effective test-taking abilities help ensure more accurate assessment of student abilities.
Notetaking and outlining	Effective note taking and outlining skills allow students to document key points of topics for future study.
Report writing	Report writing is a widely used method for documenting information and expressing ideas.
Oral presentations	Oral presentations provide students an alternative method to express themselves and report information.
Time management	Time management assists in reducing the number of unfinished assignments and facilitates more effect use of time.
Self-management	Self-management assists students in assuming responsibility for their own behaviors.
Organization	Organizational skills help in managing learning-related activities.

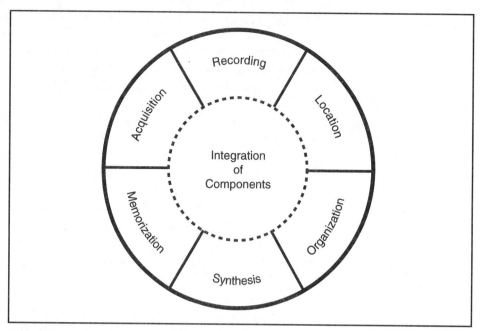

Figure 1.1. Learning components addressed through study skills.

synthesis, and memorization, as well as the integration of these components. One or more of these learning components are emphasized as students complete educational tasks. Study skills help the learner complete, adequately and efficiently, the educational tasks associated with the learning components. Thus, proficiency in the use of a variety of study skills facilitates effective mastery in the use of the learning components. In the following sections, we briefly define each of these learning components and highlight some of the study skills associated with each area. (The identified study skills are discussed more thoroughly in Chapter 5.) In addition, we provide some examples of various educational activities in the discussions of each learning component, not in an attempt to cite all possible activities, but merely to exemplify further the importance of study skills.

Acquisition

According to Polloway, Patton, and Serna (2004), acquisition refers to initially learning a skill or behavior and develops via verbal instructions, teacher demonstrations, and direct instruction to students. It is the crucial first step toward learning classroom material. This component taps several study skills, including listening, reading, and notetaking.

Recording

The recording component pertains to any classroom activity that requires the student to record responses, answers, or ideas. As recording may ensue from either written or oral forms of communication, the study skills associated with both forms become important when recording is required in a learning situation. Recording may encompass the study skills of notetaking, report writing, oral presentations, and test taking.

Location

Students employ locating skills to seek out and find information. Deshler, Ellis, and Lenz (1996) identify several activities that necessitate using location skills, including finding words in a dictionary, pursuing library research, identifying major components of a book, examining various elements of visual aids, and locating certain items in printed material (e.g., chapters; headings; page numbers; specific sentences, paragraphs, or words). This learning component incorporates several study skills, including reading rate, library usage, notetaking, reference material usage, and report writing.

Organization

The learning component of organization involves the ability to arrange and manage learning activities effectively. This component includes any educational activity or groups of activities that require student discretion relative to the organization of a completed task. With the exception of highly teacher-directed activities, organizational skills are necessary throughout the school day. Students frequently must organize their time or approach to a task when completing written assignments, oral presentations, or tests. Study skills such as reading rate, library usage, notetaking, report writing, and time management assist students in successfully completing tasks that require organization of time and approach to task completion.

Synthesis

The skill of synthesizing information, as outlined in the *Taxonomy of Educational Objectives* (Bloom, Englehart, Furst, Hill, & Krathwohl, 1956), is important in the learning process. Synthesis skills are those abilities necessary to integrate elements or parts in order to form a whole. A key factor in this component involves creating something (written or oral) that was not clearly evident prior to the synthesis of information. The process includes activities such as drawing inferences or formulating ideas from existing material, creating alternative solutions or possible options from a series of ideas or statements, making oral or written presentations of one's theory or position concerning a specific topic, and other related activities where several ideas or sources are synthesized. Although synthesizing skills often pertain to use of more complex information and learning, simplified versions of activities that draw on this learning component can be generated and used with students. The ability to synthesize information effectively taps several study skills, including reading, listening, notetaking, reference material usage, and test taking.

Memorization

Remembering previously learned material is a learning component that relies on the skills of storing and recalling or retrieving information. Various researchers have documented the problems encountered by some students as they attempt to remember information (see Polloway et al., 2004). Wallace and Kauffman (1990) wrote that some learners frequently have problems with short-term memory, which includes the ability to store and retrieve information for only a few seconds or minutes, and noted that short-term memory is essential for committing information to long-term memory successfully. Because all learned material requires the use of memory abilities, all study skills will affect, either directly or indirectly, students' abilities to remember information.

Integration of Components

The element of integration emphasizes the importance of using the various learning components together. Integration refers to one's ability to employ two or more learning components simultaneously. Although it is important for students to master each learning component as a separate activity, a more frequent occurrence is the simultaneous use of the learning components to complete educational tasks. For example, for some tasks students need to organize and record information. In other situations students may need to locate, organize, record, and synthesize information. The interrelationship among learning components as a structured whole should be emphasized to facilitate their combined use by students.

Current Issues and Study Skills

Hoover (2005) discussed a variety of current issues challenging educators of students with learning problems in today's classrooms:

- The No Child Left Behind Act of 2001 and the Individuals with Disabilities Education Improvement Act of 2004
- Inclusive education
- Three-tier instruction
- Response to Intervention
- Differentiated learning and instruction
- Accommodations and special needs
- Cultural/linguistic diversity and the education of English language learners

Each of these issues has specific implications for the need to develop and use study skills in the classroom to meet the needs of at-risk learners. The significance of study skills education relative to each issue is discussed in the following sections.

No Child Left Behind Act and IDEA

The NCLB (2001) legislation ensures that all children, including those with special needs, meet high state standards in education. Both IDEA (2004) and NCLB require that all students, including English language learners (ELLs) and those with disabilities, participate in state assessments. The law, to be implemented over a 10-year span, has specific implications for teaching study skills and strategies to students with diverse needs. As a result of NCLB, all students are expected to be educated by highly trained and qualified teachers, to be proficient in reading by the end of third grade, and to graduate from high school. In addition, all ELLs are expected to be proficient in English by the time they complete schooling.

Among the many requirements and resources for schools to use and follow, several relate specifically to study skills for students with diverse learning and behavior needs. These include the following:

1. Annual testing of proficiency toward meeting state standards
2. Use of highly qualified and well-trained professionals
3. Ongoing supplemental support and assistance for students not meeting standards
4. Accommodations to ensure opportunities to learn the mandated curricula
5. Assessment accommodations, when appropriate, for students with disabilities

The need for study skills usage to successfully implement NCLB and IDEA becomes clearer as this list is considered. Today, most states have developed some form of standards-based education (see Chapter 2), and both NCLB and IDEA require that all students be provided the opportunity to learn using the state-mandated curricula and assessment (Hoover & Patton, 2005).

Significance to Study Skills

Recent legislation highlights the need for study skills development and usage in the instruction of students with learning and behavior problems. To address NCLB and IDEA mandates in the classroom, teachers must help students to develop and use study skills so they can be successful, especially within standards-based education.

Inclusive Education

The most pervasive trend in education of students with learning problems is placement in inclusive educational settings. Inclusion presents a variety of challenges to general and special educators in their efforts to meet diverse learning and behavior needs. A primary goal of inclusion is to create an educational environment in which all students have opportunities to learn (Stainback, Stainback, East, & Sapon-Shevin, 1995).

Inclusive education has systematically evolved over the past several decades as illustrated in Table 1.2, which summarizes the predominant trends in special education placement(s), prevailing educational perspectives, and study skills implications since the 1960s. Placement patterns for special education students have moved from virtual exclusion to comprehensive inclusion in the general education classroom. Identifying the most effective educational services for students with diverse needs continues to challenge educators. The debate concerning full inclusion (all students educated in inclusive settings all the time) is far from over. However, as noted by Fuchs and Fuchs in 1994, special and inclusive educators must at minimum redefine their relationship and scope of tasks. This holds true today as schools try to meet educational challenges of the 21st century (Hoover, 2005).

Significance to Study Skills

Inclusive education affects both special and general education classroom settings in a variety of ways. One area of impact is the continued need to teach study skills and study strategies in inclusive settings. The increase in (a) the number of special learners who are educated in inclusive classes and (b) the emphasis on state-mandated curricula for all students highlights the importance for educators to work collaboratively to effectively teach students study skills and strategies.

Table 1.2
Trends in Educational Services and Placements for Students with Disabilities in Elementary and Secondary Schools

Period	Predominant Theme	Primary Placement(s)	Prevailing Thought Toward Education	Predominant View Toward Curriculum
Early 1960s	Separate special education was needed	Self-contained classroom	Students who could not benefit from general education would be best served in special classrooms.	Specialized curriculum and techniques were needed to effectively educate individuals with disabilities.
Late 1960s	Effectiveness of separate special classrooms was questioned	Self-contained classroom	Educators questioned the practice and effects of educating students with disabilities in separate special classes.	The need for special curriculum and techniques for many students with disabilities was being questioned.
1970s	Education for many students with special needs does not occur in separate classrooms	Resource rooms with some education in general education classrooms	Many learners would benefit from education in general education classrooms, requiring only some education in a special classroom.	Selected aspects of the general education curriculum were appropriate for learners with special needs.
1980s	Students with special needs may be appropriately educated in general education classrooms	General education classrooms with some education in resource rooms	The least restrictive environment for many students termed "disabled" was education in the general education classroom.	Many students would benefit from the general education curriculum if proper adaptations and modifications were provided.
1990s	Students with disabilities should achieve full inclusion into general education	Full integration into general education services and classrooms	The education of all students with disabilities would be best achieved in the general education setting.	Continued expansion of integrated programs and curricula was implemented in inclusive education settings.
2000s	Full inclusion is reaffirmed for all students	General education settings	The goal is to meet all diverse needs through differentiated instruction with special educator collaborative support.	Standards-based education and curriculum are mandated in most states for all learners.

Note: Adapted from *Curriculum Adaptations for Students with Learning and Behavior Problems: Differentiating Instruction to Meet Diverse Needs* (3rd ed., p. 29), by J. J. Hoover and J. R. Patton, 2005, Austin, TX: PRO-ED. Copyright 2005 by PRO-ED, Inc. Adapted with permission.

Teaching Study Skills to Students with Learning Problems

Three-Tier Instruction

Another important recent development in education is the implementation of three-tier or multilevel instruction. Within this type of model, three levels or tiers of instruction exist.

‖ *Tier 1. High-Quality Core Instruction:* High-quality, research-based, and systematic instruction in a challenging curriculum

‖ *Tier 2. High-Quality Targeted Supplemental Instruction:* Targeted and focused interventions to supplement core instruction

‖ *Tier 3. High-Quality Intensive Intervention:* Specialized interventions to meet significant disabilities

Within the three-tiered instructional system, the role of special education is most apparent in Tier 3 as intensive instruction is provided to special education students. However, special educators also must assume important roles in Tiers 1 and 2.

Within three-tiered instructional programming, students initially are provided high-quality core instruction (Tier 1) in the inclusive educational classroom. As "reasonable and targeted" differentiated instruction is implemented within the core instruction, some students emerge as requiring additional high-quality targeted supplemental instruction (Tier 2). This supplemental instruction

- may occur in the general education setting or other settings within the school,
- is targeted to specific areas of need, and
- directly complements the core instruction.

As evidence-based documentation and evaluation of the targeted supplemental instruction are completed, those students who continue to experience significant academic or social–emotional problems are considered for more high-quality intensive intervention (Tier 3). Estimates, particularly in the area of reading, are that approximately 80% of all learners are successful with high-quality core instruction, 15% to 20% are estimated to need targeted supplemental instruction, and 5% to 10% require intensive or special services through high-quality intensive intervention (Hasbrouck, 2002; Yell, 2004).

Significance to Study Skills

Study skills usage with students who have learning problems is essential in all three instructional levels to best meet educational needs. Students with potential learning problems may employ selected study skills and strategies to successfully deal with core instruction (Tier 1). If targeted supplemental instruction (Tier 2) is required, a greater focus and emphasis on study skills is necessary to best support learning. Continued emphasis on study skills and related life skills is necessary to address the more intensive needs of students educated in Tier 3. Overall, the development and use of study skills within three-tier instruction is critical to understanding when a learner requires Tier 2 or 3 instructional services.

Response to Intervention

According to Vaughn and Fuchs (2003), Response to Intervention is a process for determining the effectiveness of various instructional practices. Specifically,

Response to Intervention is characterized by the following principles (Vaughn & Fuchs, 2003):

- Intervention is provided early to students.
- Student needs are identified and matched to appropriate instruction.
- Instruction is implemented on a regular basis and monitored with specific documentation.
- Differentiated instruction occurs as necessary to meet diverse student needs.
- Decisions concerning student progress are based on monitored and recorded response to instruction.
- Students' need for special education assessment and/or services is based on their response to learning through the strategies and modifications implemented.

Response to Intervention is linked to three-tier instructional programming and focuses on how a student responds to learning (Hoover & Patton, 2005). Initially generated in the 1980s, Response to Intervention may also provide an alternative process for identifying learning and reading disabilities (Vaughn, Linan-Thompson, & Hickman, 2003). Currently, many educational organizations advocate and support the momentum for some form of Response to Intervention to determine eligibility for special education services (Fuchs, Mock, Morgan, & Young, 2003).

As students demonstrate failure to make adequate progress, documented through ongoing monitoring, additional modifications and strategies are implemented, with continued documentation of progress. Within the Response to Intervention process, students who fail to make satisfactory educational progress would qualify for a formal special education evaluation and/or placement services (Fuchs et al., 2003).

As a strategy for determining need for special education assessment or services, Response to Intervention has specific applications to usage of study skills and study strategies in the classroom. Specifically, the effective implementation of curriculum for students with learning and behavior problems requires ongoing modifications or adaptations to meet diverse needs. As the study skills discussed throughout this book are incorporated into differentiated learning, valuable data and information may be gathered and used to determine students' response to intervention.

Table 1.3 provides an overview of targeted study skills benchmarks used to evaluate student response to intervention for each of the 12 study skills discussed in this book. The targeted responses to learning are provided to serve as benchmarks for determining progress toward achieving effective use and application of study skills in the classroom.

Significance to Study Skills

Teachers using Response to Intervention should address how students' overall learning is affected by their application of study skills and study strategies. Educators who understand and apply the interrelationship between curriculum implementation and study skills usage are able to make more informed decisions concerning the need for special education based on a learner's response to intervention.

Differentiated Learning and Instruction

The need for differentiating or adapting curriculum and instruction for students with learning problems has existed for many years. Inclusion efforts over the

Table 1.3

Response to Intervention and Study Skills Benchmarks

Study Skill	Targeted Study Skills Response
Reading rate	Uses rate appropriate to type and length of assignment
Listening	Employs proper listening skills to understand material
Graphic aids	Uses graphic aids to better understand or clarify information
Library usage	Accesses and uses library information in learning
Reference materials usage	Uses reference sources to support learning
Test taking	Exhibits appropriate test-studying, test-taking, and reviewing skills
Notetaking and outlining	Records key points to facilitate future study and review
Report writing	Clearly expresses ideas relevant to the writing assignment
Oral presentations	Orally expresses self by clearly and coherently articulating ideas
Time management	Uses time efficiently to complete tasks and assignments
Self-management	Assumes responsibility for own learning and behaviors
Organization	Employs effective organization to facilitate successful learning

past few decades have challenged both special and inclusive educators to modify their curriculum to meet diverse needs in the classroom. The development, usage, and application of study skills and study strategies are central to effectively differentiating instruction in special and inclusive classrooms.

Although specific terminology may vary (i.e., *adaptation, differentiation, modification*), the issue for students with special needs is that curriculum, including standards-based curriculum, must be differentiated to meet diverse educational needs. Gartin, Murdick, Imbeau, and Perner (2002) describe differentiated instruction as "using strategies that address student strengths, interests, skills, and readiness in flexible learning environments" (p. 8). Differentiated instruction addresses a variety of curricular elements including content, instructional strategies, student behaviors, and the overall instructional setting (Hoover & Patton, 2005).

As teachers strive to differentiate curriculum and instruction for students with learning problems, student use of study skills must be an integral component of those modifications. Table 1.4 provides examples of how each study skill discussed in this book may be effectively included in differentiated instruction for students with special needs. An in-depth understanding of study skills development and usage in the classroom is essential to effectively differentiating curriculum and instruction for all students.

Significance to Study Skills

As learners master study skills and associated study and learning strategies, they will be better prepared for differentiated learning. This preparation is essential to meet current mandated standards-based curriculum and assessment.

Accommodations and Special Needs

Many classroom situations require the use of acceptable accommodations to ensure appropriate instruction and assessment for students with learning problems. Use of study skills in conjunction with differentiated instruction facilitates

Table 1.4
Study Skills and Differentiated Instruction

Study Skill	Considerations to Differentiate Instruction
Reading rate	Accommodate learning to reflect different reading rates appropriate to type and length of assignment
Listening	Review strategies for effective listening prior to the listening activity or lecture
Graphic aids	Create multiple uses for graphic aids in assignments to help students see the value of visual material
Library usage	Develop regular assignments to access and use library information in learning completed by teams
Reference materials usage	Incorporate and integrate reference sources to support learning in specific assignments and tasks
Test taking	Develop regular schedule to assist students to practice proper test-studying, test-taking, and review skills
Notetaking and outlining	Begin with less complex notetaking/outlining assignments and gradually increase level of difficulty
Report writing	Initially block out and practice the different elements of a writing assignment (Intro, Body, Concl)
Oral presentations	Create a flexible, non-threatening learning environment for oral presentations
Time management	Structure tasks so students must efficiently manage their time to successfully complete the assignments
Self-management	Create a flexible learning environment to allow for use of student-directed self-management techniques
Organization	Allow flexibility in how students organize their learning

higher quality education as well as more accurate assessment results. Table 1.5 provides an overview of five types of acceptable accommodations—presentation, response, time, scheduling, and setting (Thompson, 2004)—and their relevance to curriculum implementation and study skills education. Study skills that may assist with implementing these accommodations in the classroom include reading rate, test taking, time management, and self-management. As a result, study skills are also important to the successful implementation of accommodations to help students with special needs successfully learn.

Cultural/Linguistic Diversity and Study Skills

The National Research Council (Donovan & Cross, 2002) reported that English language learners (ELLs) continue to be at risk for special education placement. The inappropriate use of standardized assessment with ELLs often underestimates these students' academic progress and contributes to the risk of their overidentification for special education (Baca & Cervantes, 2004; Cummins & Sayers, 1995). In many situations, poor test results of ELLs reflect lack of proficiency in test-taking or other study skills rather than lack of content knowledge, further highlighting the importance of emphasizing study skills development for ELLs with special needs. Effective study skills education for ELLs with learning problems challenges all teachers to meet diverse needs relative to cultural and linguistic values (Hoover & Patton, 2005).

Table 1.5
Accommodations to Meet Special Needs

Accommodation	Strategy	Assessment and Curriculum Considerations	Related Study Skills
Presentation	Adjust the manner in which material is presented	Situation may require greater or lesser visual or auditory emphasis	Listening Graphic aids Oral presentations
Response	Adjust methods or manner of response needed to complete tasks	Response procedures may need to be adapted to ensure opportunity to learn and accurate test results	Test taking Notetaking or outlining Time management
Time	Break down or adjust time allotments to complete tasks	Allow time considerations that facilitate task completion while accounting for individual attention or processing abilities	Test taking Time management Self-management Organization
Scheduling	Adjust learner's schedule to reflect effective task completion and opportunities to learn	Restructure schedules for taking tests or completing assignments to best reflect student time on task, attention span, and content difficulty	Reading rate Test taking Time management Organization
Setting	Alter location or environmental conditions for completing tasks and taking tests	Differentiate classroom settings to reduce distractions and account for a variety of materials or strategies that may be required	Test taking Time management Self-management

The following principles to consider in the education of ELLs (Garcia, 2001; O'Malley & Pierce, 1996; Ovando, Collier, & Combs, 2003) also apply to an overall study skills program:

- Relate study skills to students' culture, background, environment, and prior experiences.
- Reinforce study skills over time and across subject areas.
- Help students meet cognitive and academic study skills goals in integrated ways.
- Establish high expectations for use of study skills while valuing diversity.
- Expect students to perform active learning and inquiry-based tasks while employing appropriate study skills.

Expanding upon these principles, Hoover and Patton (2005) summarize six curricular elements that a teacher must consider to effectively teach ELLs. As shown in Table 1.6, study skills usage supports these six curricular factors for

Table 1.6

Cultural and Linguistic Considerations and Study Skills
for English Language Learners (ELLs)

Curricular Factors	Overview	Study Skills Considerations
Language function	*Communicative*—Routine conversational social language *Academic*—Higher level language usage	Language usage in the classroom should support student's study skills abilities to interpret and convey meaning for authentic purposes
Acculturation	Process by which one cultural group assumes traits of another cultural group	ELLs exhibit varied responses to acculturation such as withdrawal or stress and effective use of study skills may assist to minimize these emotional responses
Conceptual knowledge	New information is built upon existing information/knowledge	ELLs prior/current conceptual knowledge is essential to develop new concepts, including use of study skills
Thinking abilities	ELL students should be challenged to use and apply higher order thinking abilities	Students use of study skills facilitates development of higher order thinking skills, providing insight as to how ELLs interact with and learn curriculum
Cultural values and norms	Students come from a variety of backgrounds, possessing varying cultural backgrounds, values, and beliefs, and they often speak different languages	Cultural values may influence how students prefer to use study skills; these values must be respected
Teaching and learning styles	Education of ELL students should focus on how the child learns and under what conditions	ELLs may use different reasoning strategies according to their native languages or cultural customs and study skills usage must support preferred styles of learning; teaching styles must not conflict with student styles

Note: From *Curriculum Adaptations for Students with Learning and Behavior Problems: Differentiating Instruction to Meet Diverse Needs* (3rd ed., p. 115), by J. J. Hoover and J. R. Patton, 2005, Austin, TX: PRO-ED. Copyright 2005 by PRO-ED, Inc. Reprinted with permission.

effective education for ELLs. Addressing these six factors when teaching study skills will help the teacher ascertain the best strategies while valuing the learner's cultural and linguistic diversity.

Study skills related to test taking are of specific significance to educating and assessing ELLs. Hoover and Trujillo-Hinsch (1999) investigated test-taking skills (test preparation, test completion—objective tests, test completion—essay tests, and test review skills) of third- and sixth-grade ELLs. Conclusions relevant to teaching study skills to these students follow. Both third- and sixth-grade ELLs

- perceive themselves as using and applying various test-studying and test-taking skills on a regular basis.
- perceive their test preparation skills to be their weakest test-taking skill.
- perceive their test completion skills to be stronger than their test preparation skills.

- seem to show little or no relationship between how well they scored on the district or state achievement tests and their perceptions of their own test-taking skills.
- appear to feel confident with specific objective and essay test-taking mechanics but lack confidence in their overall preparation to take tests.

Third-grade ELLs also had similar, positive perceptions toward their use of test-taking skills regardless of whether they were taught primarily in Spanish or in English.

Study Skills and Students with Learning Problems

In reference to study skill development and students with learning problems, Gearheart, Weishahn, and Gearheart (1996) report that students who exhibit learning problems frequently do not possess adequate study skills necessary for work in inclusive classes. Salend (2000) remarks that many students with learning problems do not possess adequate study habits and many, therefore, perform poorly. In addition, Deshler et al. (1996) suggest that adolescent students with learning disabilities generally are not taught study skills at the elementary level. Other researchers also have documented the prevalence of deficient study skills in students with special needs (Hoover, 2004a; Hoover & Collier, 1992; Hoover & Trujillo-Hinsch, 1999).

Specifically, many students with learning problems have deficient notetaking, listening, test-taking, organization, and scanning skills. Smith, Polloway, Patton, and Dowdy (2000) assert that adolescents with learning problems often experience difficulty in organizing information while taking notes. Mercer and Mercer (2000) have documented deficient test-taking skills in students with high-incidence disabilities, noting that these learners may experience difficulty adapting to the format and tasks associated with standardized achievement tests. Also, elementary students with learning or behavior problems often experience test-taking problems (Hoover, 2004b). Thus, the importance of study skills, along with the difficulties that many students with learning problems experience in employing them, suggest the need for an increased emphasis on the development and maintenance of effective study skills usage in programs for students with learning problems in elementary and secondary education.

Need for Developing Study Skills

Although the specific use of study skills generally occurs at school and during school-related tasks, the development of these skills contributes to the overall growth of learners as they prepare for dealing with the demands of adulthood. Because study skills are important both for the completion of school tasks and for the overall development of independent functioning, teachers must be involved in helping learners acquire and maintain study skills usage. Students must develop and use study skills to

- Complete assignments efficiently and effectively
- Minimize wasted time in school
- Complete work on time

- Get the most out of any particular assignment
- Complete tasks independently
- Take charge of their own learning
- Be responsible for their own learning
- Proofread and review work carefully prior to submission to the instructor
- Plan and carry out daily, weekly, or monthly schedules effectively
- Make complex assignments less cumbersome and more manageable
- Complete homework
- Work with other classmates

In many situations, the completion of daily classroom assignments, weekly tests, semester term papers, or homework assignments may be improved if students possess and apply a variety of study skills. Moreover, the successful use of such skills is requisite for students in inclusive settings. Better students possess and employ study skills effectively and on a regular basis.

Understanding Study Skills Programs in School

Many different study skills programs may exist in schools, and the extent to which study skills are emphasized varies from teacher to teacher and classroom to classroom. Some study skills, such as use of reference materials and interpreting graphic or visual material, are emphasized in numerous classrooms, especially during reading-related opportunities. However, many other such skills also must be addressed and included in daily teaching activities. Although study skills programs vary by classroom and grade level, some general characteristics should be included in most study skills programs:

- Simple variations of the different study skills should be introduced in the early grades.
- More complex variations of study skills should be introduced gradually as students progress through the grades.
- Specific goals and objectives for study skills programs should be identified prior to beginning such a program and revised as the needs of students dictate.
- Learner strengths regarding study skills usage should be emphasized, and direct instruction should be given in areas of weakness.
- The proper uses of each study skill should be explained and demonstrated to students.
- Continued opportunity for use of specific study skills should be provided to students to improve and maintain proficiency.
- The teaching and use of study skills should occur within context in the classroom as different opportunities arise, rather than only as isolated courses of study in which selected study skills are periodically emphasized.

Perhaps the greatest key to understanding study skills programs in school is the fact that these skills can and must be *taught*; students typically do not develop study skills without some instruction. The development of such skills is not a naturally occurring event as students progress through school.

2

Study Skills and Standards-Based Education

To meet the demands of standards-based initiatives, study skills use by students with learning and behavior problems becomes increasingly more important.

The No Child Left Behind Act of 2001 requires that all students, including those with disabilities, be assessed through state assessments. As the act is implemented in states and schools, curricula must reflect state standards and all students must be taught the knowledge and skills associated with the standards. This chapter includes discussion of meeting special needs in standards-based curriculum, aligning study skills development with standards-based curriculum, and achieving study skills teaching competence necessary to effectively educate students with special needs through a standards-based curriculum.

Standards-Based Education and Meeting Special Needs

Standards-based curriculum was initially introduced in the 1970s through the reform movement stressing minimum competencies. Although the current reforms reflect these prior efforts, the assessment of the proficiency levels of the standards has changed from simply pass or fail to multiple proficiency levels (e.g., *not proficient, partially proficient, proficient*) (Linn & Herman, 1997). In addition, standards must be written so everyone, including parents, understands learner expectations (Education Commission of the States, 2003). As a result, an interconnectedness exists among standards, curriculum implementation, and assessment.

Significant evolution in the development of standards-based education has occurred in assessment associated with instruction (i.e., standards-based assessment designed to identify levels of proficiency). To effectively implement standards-based curriculum, instructors must teach study skills relative to the specific structure and intent of the standards. Table 2.1, developed from Hoover and Patton (2005) and Linn and Herman (1997), identifies several elements of standards-based education and implications for study skills development.

Standards-based reforms provide educators an opportunity to reverse the trend of lowering standards for students with special needs, because educators now must do whatever is necessary to help students achieve proficiency of standards. Rather than lowering the standards for students with special needs, educators are held accountable to raise their expectations and associated teaching competence to meet standards. According to Maccini and Gagnon (2002), however, both inclusive and special educators stated that a major barrier to successful implementation of standards-based curriculum is the lack of adequate resources and materials. Standards-based curriculum provides a clear direction toward what students should learn, which results in the need for teachers to adapt and modify instruction, as well as emphasize study skills and learning strategies, to ensure that all students have sufficient opportunities to learn the content and skills associated with each standard (Quenemoen, Lehr, Thurlow, & Massanaair, 2001).

The study skills and learning strategies discussed in this book are most appropriate to meeting standards-based curricular demands to successfully educate all students, including students with special needs. As elementary and secondary teachers implement the 12 study skills presented in this book, they have the best opportunity of meeting the diverse educational needs of all learners within the broader context of standards-based education and assessment.

The need for teachers to become competent with teaching study skills within standards-based education is as important as it has ever been for students with diverse needs. Figure 2.1 summarizes the importance of study skills in the overall education of standards-based learning within the context of the three standards elements: content, performance, and opportunities to learn. *Content standards* refer to subject area skills and knowledge; *performance standards* address profi-

Table 2.1

Elements of Standards-Based Education and Study Skills Implications

Elements of Standards-Based Education	Study Skills Implications
Close link between assessment and curriculum	A significant alignment exists between the curriculum being taught and the skills and knowledge being assessed.
	Study skills must support this alignment by reinforcing tools for learning standards-based curriculum content.
Comparison of student's proficiency to standards, not to other students' proficiency	Standards-based curriculum stresses the development of standards, and assessment results reflect the level of proficiency for each student. Thus, the assessment compares students' proficiency levels with established standards and not with other students' proficiency levels.
	Study skills assist learners to self-monitor their progress toward achieving standards.
Use of alternative assessments	Assessment of standards-based curriculum may include a variety of assessment strategies, such as constructed response, essays, authentic and real-life problem solving, and rubrics.
	Study skills usage allows learners to demonstrate in alternative ways their proficiency levels associated with standards.
Achieving proficiency	The No Child Left Behind Act of 2001 requires that states and school systems annually monitor progress toward helping all students achieve proficiency of the standards, rather than simply reporting grouped, grade-level scores.
	Study skills development directly supports student efforts to achieve knowledge and skills learned through standards-based curriculum.
Application of results	Standards-based assessment results can be used to determine graduation requirements, hold educators accountable, and adapt curriculum. Results are no longer simply reported; rather, they are used for program improvement and documentation of progress toward full proficiency.
	Development and application of study skills should be monitored on a regular basis to complement monitoring efforts of progress toward standards proficiency.
Inclusion of all students	Standards-based curriculum is designed to challenge all students, including English language learners and students with disabilities, to increase their expectations and proficiency levels.
	Study skills provide all students with diverse needs increased opportunities to learn effectively to be successful in standards-based education.

ciency levels of performance; and *opportunities to learn standards* include various materials, management skills, strategies, and structure necessary for learning to best occur (Hoover & Patton, 2004; McLaughlin & Shepard, 1995).

The effective use of study skills assists learners to best meet the different standards elements. For example, study skills such as reading rate, listening, graphic aids, and use of reference materials directly help students learn content knowledge and skills standards. Performance standards are directly impacted by the study skills of test taking, report writing, and notetaking. In addition, as students improve their study skills in time management, self-management, and organization, their opportunities to learn are increased, which have a direct impact on the content and performance standards. As a result, the implementation of a comprehensive study skills program assists educators to prepare students with learning and behavior problems to succeed in standards-based education. In summary, the development, implementation, and application of a variety of study skills contributes to effective standards-based learning in integrative ways.

Aligning Study Skills Development with Standards

Study skills development and usage for students with learning and behavior problems must occur more frequently to ensure successful standards-based teaching and learning. An understanding of the process for aligning standards and curriculum, along with implications for study skills alignment, provides valuable insight into how to teach study skills to students with learning and behavior problems within standards-based education.

A study skills program must support each of the three standards presented in Figure 2.1 (content, performance, and opportunities to learn) to best teach standards-

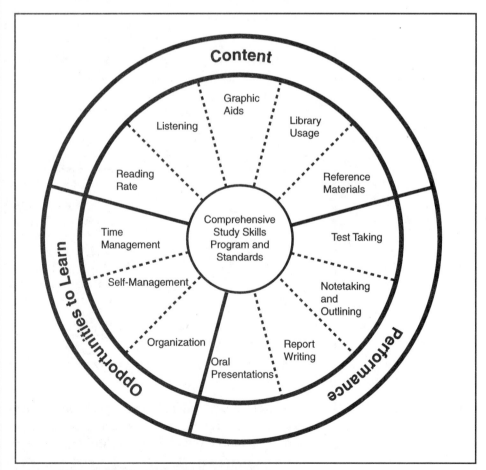

Figure 2.1. Standards elements and study skills usage.

based curriculum to students with learning and behavior problems. Table 2.2 summarizes a process to follow in planning and implementing a comprehensive study skills program within a standards-based curriculum for Grades K–12. The process for aligning study skills with standards-based curriculum follows a sequence similar to other curriculum development and reform efforts. Adhering to the phases identified in Table 2.2 will ensure that study skills become integral to standards-based education. Also, when aligning study skills usage in standards-based education, each of the study skills must be addressed and considered relative to each other. Table 2.3 illustrates examples of benchmarks for each study skill. As shown, benchmarks for each of the 12 study skills should be considered and addressed to ensure comprehensive and interrelated implementation of a study skills program within standards-based education.

Study Skills Teaching Competence

All elementary and secondary teachers of students who have learning or behavior problems must teach study skills and assist students to apply them in actual classroom situations and tasks. Throughout this book we present many strategies, concepts, and suggestions for teaching and developing student study skills. Due to the significance of study skills in teaching and learning, all educators should strive to achieve full competence in teaching study skills to meet diverse needs in their

Table 2.2

Phases in the Alignment of Study Skills with Standards-Based Curriculum

Phase	Related Action
1. Planning	Identify needs, resources, and skills required to effectively align study skills with standards. This phase includes determining which standards should be included in the alignment, procedures for alignment, and timelines.
2. Needs Assessment	Complete a needs assessment of the existing curriculum to determine how and to what extent study skills are currently addressed and taught.
3. Development	Infuse study skills and their usage into the curriculum. This includes developing performance standards and ensuring that students have sufficient opportunities to acquire, master, and generalize study skills associated with the standards.
4. Pilot	Field test the newly revised curriculum to ensure that all study skills to be included in the alignment have been infused into the curriculum. Evaluation of the pilot should address the extent to which the content, performance, and opportunities to learn standards are supported by student usage of study skills.
5. Revise	Based on feedback obtained from the pilot, identify and incorporate any necessary revisions to alignment of study skills within the curriculum.
6. Implementation	Begin full-scale implementation of newly aligned curriculum with study skills development. The implementation should be evaluated as the pilot was.
7. Adaptations	Differentiate study skills education to meet the diverse needs of students with learning and behavior problems as they achieve proficiency with the three types of standards (content, performance, and opportunities to learn).

Table 2.3
Study Skills Benchmarks Within Standards-Based Curriculum

Study Skill	Student Benchmarks
Reading rate	Uses reading rate appropriate to type and length of assignment on a consistent, daily basis
Listening	Employs proper listening skills to understand material and demonstrates mastery of the material
Graphic aids	Uses graphic aids to understand or clarify information in all subjects and in oral and written presentations
Library usage	Accesses and uses library information in learning (including the Internet and other electronic forms)
Reference materials	Effectively uses reference sources to support learning and properly documents reference materials
Test taking	Exhibits appropriate test-studying, test-taking, and reviewing skills in all test-taking situations
Notetaking and outlining	Records all key points to facilitate future study and review; uses recorded notes in assignments
Report writing	Clearly expresses ideas in writing assignments (includes introduction, thesis, body, and conclusion elements)
Oral presentations	Orally expresses self by clearly and coherently articulating ideas verbally
Time management	Uses time efficiently to complete all tasks and assignments on a daily basis
Self-management	Assumes responsibility for own learning and behaviors; maintains effective self-control
Organization	Effectively organizes learning tasks and requirements

classrooms. Competence in teaching study skills within standards-based curriculum and assessment is achieved when the educator is knowledgeable of and proficient with the competencies presented in Table 2.4. The development of effective study skills teaching and learning requires ongoing progress and growth toward proficiency of these competencies. Study skills teaching competence ensures that all students are given the best opportunity to succeed with the ever-increasing demands placed on them to complete rigorous, mandated standards-based curricula by emphasizing appropriate and relevant study strategies.

Table 2.4
Competencies Needed To Teach Study Skills

Development Competencies	Implementation Competencies
Knowledge of	*Knowledge of*
Process for study skills development and usage	Study skills matching each student's learning styles
Study skill issues and their implications for students with special needs	Various classroom-based assessments to monitor progress with study skills usage
Appropriate study skills by age, grade, and learning strengths	Study skills instructional methods most relevant to the learner
Study skills needing to be taught, ways to teach them, and the class settings used	Strategies for differentiating the learning environment to reflect implementation of study skills
Least intrusive study skills or strategies for the learning situation	Study skills usage to facilitate maintenance and generalization of content knowledge and skills
Interrelatedness of study skills with content, materials, instructional strategies, and instructional settings	Collaboration skills to facilitate study skills usage in the inclusive education setting
Value of culture and language diversity in teaching and learning study skills	Professional advocacy for all students to appropriately use study skills to meet diverse classroom needs

Note: Adapted from information found in Hoover and Collier (2003) and Hoover and Patton (2005).

3

Study Skills and Lifelong Learning

The acquisition, use, and generalization of study skills have a direct impact on the development of life skills necessary to successfully confront daily challenges.

Effective use of study skills allows students to learn in the most efficient manner possible, whether the learning relates to school or to independent living in general. Teachers in elementary and secondary grades should have some organized program to assist students in acquiring, using, and maintaining study skills. The best programs include provisions in which ongoing development occurs through the integrated use of study skills in each content area and other daily required tasks. Teachers should begin to emphasize each of the 12 study skills in the early elementary grades, help students maintain the skills through middle school and refine the study skills usage during high school, and then help students generalize these skills into adult contexts. This developmental progression, shown in Figure 3.1, allows for structured and systematic introduction, maintenance, and generalization of study skills abilities, to facilitate students' growth toward independent learning through high school and college as well as independence in daily living.

Developing study skills at school, which leads to lifelong learning, should include the following types of teacher activities:

- Discuss different study skills with students to help them see the skills' importance in learning and in completing assigned tasks.
- Discuss with students how they approach different learning tasks and explore their use of different study skills.
- Demonstrate the proper use of needed study skills.
- Discuss with learners their completed assignments and tests on a regular basis to help them see why using different study skills contributes to correct responses.
- Point out and discuss apparent study skill errors from the results of completed assignments and tests.
- Emphasize the importance of study skills as a means of assuming responsibility for one's own learning.
- Encourage and help students to plan, organize, and evaluate their use of study skills in completing assigned work.

As students progress through school, their continued use of study skills allows them to become more responsible for their own learning and facilitates the proper development and application of study habits beyond secondary education.

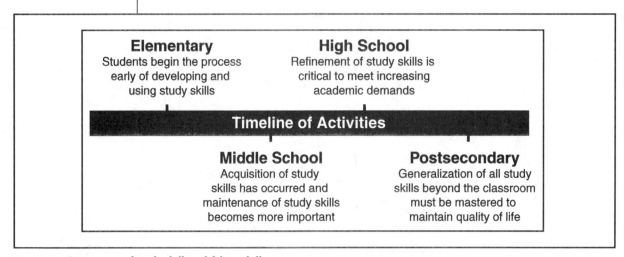

Figure 3.1. Continuum of study skills as lifelong skills.

Early Development of Study Skills

Although the use of study skills is most reflected in upper elementary and secondary education literature and books, the reality is that, unless a basic study skills foundation is laid in early elementary school, many students will experience difficulty with study skills at the time they are most needed. In addition, it is misguided to believe that only students in upper elementary and secondary education are capable of learning study skills. Further, educators should not ignore the fact that students in lower elementary grades, just like those in upper elementary and secondary schooling, are required to engage activities such as these:

- Completing tests
- Doing homework
- Writing reports
- Listening to the teacher instruct
- Using a library
- Locating and using reference materials
- Managing and organizing time
- Managing own behaviors

Study skills are "tools" that any learner may use to complete tasks and assignments. Although some, if not many, of the structured study strategies discussed in this book may be too complex for students in the lower elementary grades, appropriate modifications of these can easily be made to facilitate the development of a sound study skills base in the lower grades. Table 3.1 provides examples of early development of study skills to build a solid foundation for later use. As shown, examples of study skills development in early elementary grades are presented. It is important for teachers to use these types of activities on a regular basis to help students in the lower grades to develop a solid foundation for study skills on which to build as they move into upper elementary and secondary grades.

Lifelong Importance of Study Skills

As we have stated, study skills are not only for students at the secondary level. Furthermore, the notion that these skills are appropriate only in an academic context provides too restricted a view of their importance in that it ignores the everyday events of living. For example, techniques that assist one in understanding written material more effectively, managing time more efficiently, or remembering information more consistently are immediately relevant to situations outside the classroom.

Table 3.2 exemplifies the link between the academic support function and the lifelong applications for each study skill discussed in this book. The intent of this table is to stress the common usage of study skills in and out of the classroom. Competence in these study skills can contribute to success in dealing with the major demands of employment and further education, home and family, leisure pursuits, community participation, physical and emotional health, and personal responsibility and relationships (Cronin, Patton, & Wood, 2006).

Learning study skills has immediate (school success) and subsequent (successful adult functioning) value. Teachers should stress the benefits of learning

(continues on pg. 31)

Table 3.1

Developing the Foundation for Study Skills in Early Elementary Grades

Study Skills	Early Development Considerations
Reading rate	Rates of reading relate specifically to reading purposes. As students begin to read or are read to, help them to listen or read for different purposes (pleasure, identifying main character, etc.).
Listening	List and post Good Listener Skills in the classroom. Be certain to include and discuss the difference between *hearing* something and *understanding* what is heard. Periodically stop verbal discussions or instructions and ask students to state what is being talked about and how it relates to the topic at hand.
Graphic aids	Studying pictures is one of the first ways children learn about different topics (e.g., items in a forest) as well as to support writing text (i.e., picture clues). Activities that combine pictures with simple text help students in early grades to develop an appreciation for use of graphic material, not only in reading but also in making oral presentations.
Library usage	Most but not all students have some experience with the elementary school's library. The foundation for library usage can easily be strengthened in early elementary school through simple tasks that require students to use the library to locate a book, resource, map, or other library material. These types of activities should be encouraged to begin the process of using a library effectively.
Reference materials	Teachers should provide students in early elementary school with tasks that require locating and using simple reference materials, including using the World Wide Web. Providing activities that require use of dictionaries and encyclopedias written for lower elementary grades assists in building a solid foundation for more complex uses of reference materials in later grades.
Test taking	Students in any grade are subjected to some form of testing in the classroom. Early support for test-taking skills in the early elementary grades should include the development and posting of three graphic aids: (a) How to study for a test, (b) How to take a test, and (c) Reviewing a graded test. Each poster should depict (in written and/or graphic form) two or three main items associated with the topic so all students in the class understand the items. These posters should be reviewed regularly.
Notetaking and outlining	Critical to effective notetaking and outlining is the ability to recognize and record essential information in an organized manner. In early elementary school, use of semantic webs or graphic organizers helps students explore essential aspects of a topic and then record this information in an organized manner, providing a foundation for more complex notetaking and outlining tasks in the future.
Report writing	Written reports provide students opportunities to discuss, evaluate, or explore a topic in writing. A variety of tasks helps students in early elementary grades to begin to develop these skills, including use of cloze procedures, sentence completion activities, or language experience tasks.

(continues)

Teaching Study Skills to Students with Learning Problems

Table 3.1 *Continued.*
Developing the Foundation for Study Skills in Early Elementary Grades

Study Skills	Early Development Considerations
Oral presentations	An underlying skill needed to successfully give oral presentations is the ability to speak in front of others to formally share ideas or information. A variety of tasks in early elementary school facilitate initial development of this study skill, including reporting orally about lessons learned on a field trip, experiences during a summer vacation, or briefly sharing a talent or hobby.
Time management	Effective use of time becomes more important as learners experience increased workloads and responsibilities; however, simple yet effective time management skills can be acquired in lower elementary grades. Examples include development of brief daily schedules with associated times; posting and periodically reviewing a time management poster with two to three easy-to-understand tips; posting the daily tasks along with beginning and ending times; or providing students with two tasks that must be completed within a specific time.
Self-management	Keeping one's behavior under control is an expectation of all students beginning with the first day they enter a formal school setting. An effective strategy for helping early elementary students with self-management is teaching the use of self-monitoring techniques. This method is easily adapted to meet younger students' needs and helps learners become more aware of their own behaviors.
Organization	Similar to time management, organizing one's learning becomes more important as workloads and responsibilities increase. Helping students develop and use a simple organization chart documenting daily tasks helps young students begin the process of developing effective organizational skills.

Table 3.2

Examples of Study Skills Functions in and out of the Classroom

Study Skill	School Examples	Life Skills Applications
Reading rate	Reviewing an assigned reading for a test	Reviewing an automobile insurance policy
	Looking for an explanation of a concept discussed in class	Reading the newspaper
Listening	Understanding instructions about a field trip	Understanding how a newly purchased appliance works
	Attending to morning announcements	Comprehending a radio traffic report
Graphic aids	Setting up the equipment of a chemistry experiment based on a diagram	Understanding the weather map in the newspaper
	Locating the most densely populated regions of the world on a map	Deciphering the store map in a mall
Library usage	Using picture files	Obtaining travel resources (books, videos)
	Searching a computerized catalog	Viewing current periodicals
Reference materials	Accessing CD-ROM encyclopedias	Using the yellow pages to locate a repair service
	Using a thesaurus to write a paper	Ordering from a mail-order catalog
Test taking	Developing tactics for retrieving information for a closed-book test	Preparing for a driver's license renewal test
	Comparing notes with textbook content	Participating in television self-tests
Notetaking and outlining	Capturing information given by a teacher on how to dissect a frog	Writing directions to a party
	Framing the structure of a paper	Planning a summer vacation
Report writing	Developing a book report	Completing the personal goals section on a job application
	Completing a science project on a specific marine organism	Writing a complaint letter
Oral presentations	Delivering a personal opinion on a current issue for a social studies class	Describing car problems to a mechanic
	Describing the results of a lab experiment	Asking a supervisor for time off from work
Time management	Allocating a set time for homework	Maintaining a daily "to do" list
	Organizing a file system for writing a paper	Avoiding overscheduling of activities
Self-management	Assuring that homework is signed by parents	Regulating a daily exercise program
	Rewarding oneself for controlling temper	Evaluating the quality of a home repair
Organization	Managing multiple tasks	Keeping organized records for tax purposes
	Organizing one's locker	Balancing work and leisure time

Teaching Study Skills to Students with Learning Problems

study skills. In working with students who have learning problems, teachers need to help students understand how these skills can be generalized to careers.

Transitioning to Life Careers

The study skills, study strategies, and learning competencies discussed throughout this book will help students with learning problems make the critical transition from secondary education to either postsecondary education or the workplace. Cohen and Spenciner (2005) identified various life or career competencies necessary for success beyond secondary education, including the following:

- Recognizing various aspects of career development
- Self-evaluating one's self-concept
- Assessing own work habits and interests
- Developing practices that promote self-development
- Evaluating results from tasks and related assessments
- Matching own interests with current abilities
- Determining work-related behaviors important for success
- Recognizing the importance of continuing with self-education and lifelong learning

As students use and develop various study skills throughout school, these and similar life skills are developed. To succeed in today's ever-changing world, students must learn to make informed decisions, manage their time and workloads, gather necessary information to make decisions, and efficiently organize themselves and their daily lives. Table 3.3 illustrates how the 12 study skills covered in this book might be needed in the workplace. Overall, students must learn how to deal with a variety of social and workplace situations in socially acceptable ways.

Life Skills, Study Skills, and Learning Components

As discussed in Chapter 1, several learning components are directly affected by the development and use of study skills. These are acquisition, recording, location, organization, synthesis, and memorization (see Figure 1.1). Life skills also are integrated directly into student development of the six learning components. Learning best occurs through the application and generalization of the learning components; that is, as students acquire, maintain, and generalize study skills, they are further developing effective usage of the learning components. This directly contributes to the student's lifelong learning because application and usage of the learning components are critical in daily living.

Table 3.3
Study Skills in the Workplace

Study Skill	How It Might Be Needed in the Workplace
Reading rate	Skimming long reports Scanning a manual for special directions
Listening	Determining key activities at weekly team meeting
Graphic aids	Using a diagram in a manual
Library usage	Acquiring journal article on a current topic being investigated
Reference materials	Locating information about a specific client
Test taking	Taking a test for a promotion to a new position
Notetaking and outlining	Recording details at a training on using a new software
Report writing	Preparing a report or proposal
Oral presentations	Sharing information learned at a recent training
Time management	Determining the timeline on a project or assignment
Self-management	Keeping one on task when working on multiple projects
Organization	Maintaining an organized work area so that key resources can be retrieved easily

CHAPTER

4

Classroom Assessment and Implementation of Study Skills

Ongoing and authentic classroom-based assessment of study skills usage must occur to determine students' response to instruction and effectiveness of a study skills program in the classroom.

This chapter explores the informal assessment of study skills and describes sample standards-based IEP goals and objectives for each of the 12 study skills discussed in this book. In addition, guidelines for planning and implementing a study skills program in the classroom are presented. The chapter also explores the use of cooperative learning and semantic webbing to help students who have learning difficulties apply study skills in the classroom and their learning.

Informal Assessment of Study Skills

To assess study skills, many educators need to develop their own informal checklists or adapt commercially available teacher-made checklists (see, e.g., Form 4.1). McLaughlin and Lewis (2000) suggested that teacher-made devices are a quick and efficient way to gather information and to identify areas that require further assistance. When developing or adapting a checklist and conducting informal assessments of study skills, the teacher should consider these steps:

1. Identify those study skills necessary to complete the assigned tasks or courses of study.
2. Construct or adapt a checklist to assess needed study skills.
3. Construct a self-analysis checklist (similar to teacher's list in Item 2) for students to complete.
4. Develop and implement evaluative activities that require use of the desired study skills.
5. Observe students during these activities, record results, and have students complete self-analysis forms.
6. Compare results from teacher and student checklists.

Figure 4.1 illustrates this assessment process. Adhering to these steps will provide some structure to the informal assessment process and enable classroom teachers to efficiently and effectively gather necessary information regarding student study skills proficiency levels.

The Study Skills Inventory (Form 4.1) lists some major subskills associated with each main study skill discussed in this book. This inventory, which may be used in conjunction with the steps outlined above, is designed to identify the perceptions of teachers and students concerning the development and use of each study skill. Considering each subskill equips teachers and students to understand those study skills that require additional development versus those that are already mastered and retained. Each subskill is important and should be addressed if not already mastered.

The inventory may be completed separately or jointly by teachers and students and should be followed by a discussion of each person's perceptions concerning mastery of each subskill. A comparison between teacher and student perceptions of study skills abilities is important. Discrepancies between documented perceptions and actual performance in school should also be discussed. Unmastered subskills associated with the study skills of immediate importance in school should be emphasized initially.

The summary section at the end of the Study Skills Inventory provides a way to analyze student competence of the various study skills areas. Each study skill area is listed along with the number of items on the scale for this area. To best understand a student's levels of proficiency, write the number of items associated with each response option for each study skill area. Assuming that responses were entered for all items within an area, the numbers entered under each of the col-

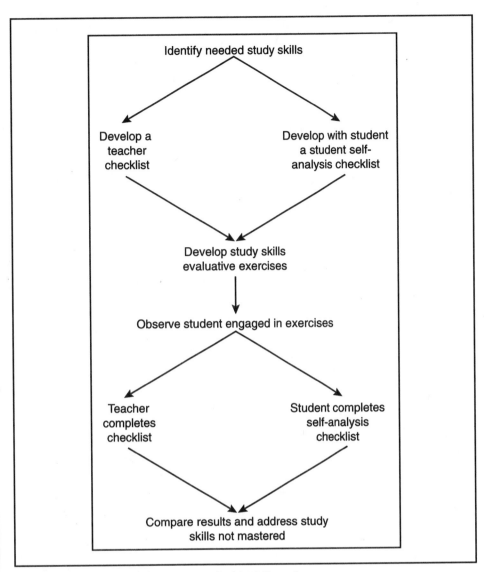

Figure 4.1. Steps to informal assessment of study skills proficiency.

umns (NP, PP, P, HP) should total the number in parentheses. After these data are charted, a teacher can easily recognize those study skills needing attention.

Teachers will need to emphasize different study skills as school demands and assignments change. For example, an upcoming test will require an emphasis on test-taking skills, and a new lecture situation will require specific attention to notetaking or outlining abilities. The Study Skills Inventory may be completed in its entirety or in selected sections to meet changing study skill demands. It may also be used in conjunction with other guides presented in this book or with other commercial study skills devices. This instrument helps teachers and students gain a general overview of study skills abilities and usage, and it provides a beginning point in the development of an effective study skills program in the classroom.

Planning To Meet Diverse Learning Needs

As part of an overall classroom study skills program, teachers must identify the skill areas that students have mastered and not mastered. Thereafter, those skills needing attention should become target areas addressed in the students' program and in the Individualized Education Programs (IEPs) of students placed in special education. Some sample IEP standards and objectives for each of the 12 specific study skills discussed in this book appear in Table 4.1. Although these represent only some of the many goals and objectives that could be developed, the important point is that study skills can and should be included in educational programs and in the IEPs of students with learning problems.

The ultimate usage of study skills by students is enhanced when teachers adhere to the following planning and implementation process, which should lead to educational programming and study skills instruction.

1. Identify the study skill(s) the student must master based on tasks that require immediate attention. (The number of study skills emphasized at one time should be kept to a minimum to ensure success.)
2. Identify the specific components within the study skill area(s) targeted in Step 1. (Mastery of subcomponents facilitates mastery of the overall study skill.)
3. Identify specific strategies for helping the student to acquire the study skill(s) and its subcomponents documented in Steps 1 and 2.
4. Provide timelines for the student to develop competence in a specific study skill.
5. Identify mastery levels expected of the student with regard to the study skill.
6. Provide evaluation procedures to determine mastery of the study skill.

As discussed previously, study skills of immediate importance should be emphasized initially. Some emphasis also should be given to a couple of associated skill areas. This ensures that only a small number of study skills are addressed at any one time and that related skills are addressed when optimally appropriate. The need to place emphasis on different skills will change as class situations change; however, the broad, long-term goal is to address each of the study skills in detail to ensure mastery through intensive study as well as through continued and generalized practice of previously mastered study skills.

Implementing a Study Skills Program

According to Hoover (2004b), a program that promotes study skills generally introduces simple variations of study skills in the primary grades and gradually increases complexity as students progress through school (see Figure 3.1 in Chapter 3). Although the levels of complexity that pertain to the various study skills taught vary with each learner's age, ability, and individual needs, early efforts to promote and teach study skills may prove beneficial over both the short- and long-term educational program because problems with study skills become more apparent as students progress through school.

As previously emphasized, study skills are employed by students in confronting various educational tasks. The selection and subsequent use of the different study strategies depend heavily on the specific skill area requiring attention, as well as on consideration of the process associated with the desired study skill. When implementing a study skills program in the classroom, the teacher must consider both the *process* the student must follow as well as the *appropriateness* of the study skill to particular educational tasks and settings. Considering these important factors may minimize the selection and use of inappropriate study strategies by the learner, which in turn will facilitate more effective student study skills usage as the more appropriate strategies are called on to confront different educational situations.

Table 4.1

Sample IEP Standards and Objectives

Standard 1. Improve usage of different reading rates
OBJECTIVE: The learner will . . .
1.1 Skim to grasp the general idea of the material
1.2 Scan to search for a specific item or piece of information
1.3 Use rapid reading to obtain main idea of selection
1.4 Use normal rate of reading to identify specific details
1.5 Use study-type reading to master details and evaluate ideas
1.6 Demonstrate the importance of using each reading rate

Standard 2. Improve ability to listen in learning situations
OBJECTIVE: The learner will . . .
2.1 Apply meaning to verbal messages
2.2 Demonstrate an understanding of verbal messages
2.3 Filter out auditory or visual distractions
2.4 Demonstrate an understanding of the importance of good listening skills in learning

Standard 3. Improve ability to understand and use graphic aid materials
OBJECTIVE: The learner will . . .
3.1 Attend to relevant elements of the visual material
3.2 Use visuals appropriately in reports and presentations
3.3 Develop own graphic aids
3.4 Demonstrate an understanding of the importance of graphic aids in learning

Standard 4. Improve abilities to use a library
OBJECTIVE: The learner will . . .
4.1 Use cataloguing system effectively (card or computerized)
4.2 Locate library materials efficiently
4.3 Understand the organizational layout of the school or classroom library
4.4 Use the school library media specialist when necessary
4.5 Know the overall functions and purposes of a library
4.6 Demonstrate an understanding of the importance of library usage skills

Standard 5. Improve abilities to use reference materials and sources
OBJECTIVE: The learner will . . .
5.1 Identify different aspects of various reference materials (index, headings, etc.)
5.2 Use guide words appropriately
5.3 Consult reference materials when necessary
5.4 Use reference materials to complete research assignments
5.5 Know different types of reference materials and sources (encyclopedia, atlas, Internet, etc.)
5.6 Demonstrate an understanding of the importance of reference materials

Standard 6. Improve test-taking abilities
OBJECTIVE: The learner will . . .
6.1 Study for tests in an organized manner
6.2 Spend appropriate amounts of time studying for different types of tests and test topics
6.3 Avoid cramming for tests
6.4 Organize narrative responses appropriately
6.5 Read and understand test directions prior to answering questions
6.6 Proofread narrative responses prior to submission of test
6.7 Identify and use clue words in questions
6.8 Properly record test responses
6.9 Save difficult items until last when taking a test
6.10 Eliminate obviously wrong answers
6.11 Systematically review completed tests to identify test-studying and test-taking errors
6.12 Correct previous test-studying and test-taking errors
6.13 Demonstrate an understanding of the importance of test-taking skills

(continues)

Table 4.1 *Continued.*
Sample IEP Standards and Objectives

Standard 7.	Improve ability to document and record key points of a topic through notetaking and outlining

OBJECTIVE: The learner will . . .

7.1 Use headings and subheadings appropriately
7.2 Take clear and concise notes from a lecture or reading material
7.3 Record all essential information about a topic
7.4 Use notetaking and outlining skills during report-writing and listening activities
7.5 Develop organized notes
7.6 Follow a consistent notetaking format
7.7 Demonstrate an understanding of the importance of effective notetaking and outlining skills

Standard 8. Improve abilities to write reports and research papers
OBJECTIVE: The learner will . . .

8.1 Organize thoughts in writing
8.2 Complete written reports from an outline
8.3 Include only necessary information in written reports
8.4 Use proper sentence structure
8.5 Use correct grammar
8.6 Use proper punctuation
8.7 Proofread written assignments prior to submission
8.8 State a clear introductory statement in written reports
8.9 Include clear concluding statements
8.10 Demonstrate an understanding of the importance of report-writing skills

Standard 9. Improve ability to make oral presentations
OBJECTIVE: The learner will . . .

9.1 Freely participate in oral presentations and discussions
9.2 Adequately prepare for oral presentations
9.3 Present an organized oral presentation
9.4 Speak clearly during oral discussions
9.5 Demonstrate an understanding of the importance of oral presentation skills

(continues)

Hoover (2004b) outlines several guidelines for teachers to follow when developing and implementing a study skills program. Although many ideas appear throughout this book, several guidelines are of particular importance and should be highlighted here. These guidelines may serve as a basis for structuring the appropriate selection and usage of different strategies in the classroom, plus they may also be used in conjunction with the cooperative learning and assessment procedures discussed in this chapter. Although applicable to most learners, these guidelines are presented relative to the education of students who have learning problems. Although the guidelines are interrelated when used in actual practice, they appear separately here to highlight important points regarding each.

‖ *Guideline 1: Establish and define specific goals for your study skills program.* This process involves defining specific study skills program goals and then breaking them down into manageable daily and weekly objectives. Specific goals may include provisions for improving, for example, test-taking abilities, notetaking and outlining skills, appropriate use of various reading rates, and effective time management. Implied in this particular guideline is the importance of knowing why specific goals have been selected as part of the study skills program. Decisions

Table 4.1 *Continued.*
Sample IEP Standards and Objectives

Standard 10. Improve abilities to manage time effectively
OBJECTIVE: The learner will . . .
10.1 Complete tasks on time
10.2 Plan and organize daily activities and responsibilities effectively
10.3 Plan and organize weekly and monthly schedules effectively
10.4 Reorganize priorities as necessary
10.5 Meet scheduled deadlines
10.6 Accurately perceive the amount of time required to complete tasks
10.7 Adjust time allotments for specific tasks as necessary
10.8 Accept responsibility for managing own time
10.9 Demonstrate an understanding of the importance of effective time management

Standard 11. Improve abilities to manage own behavior
OBJECTIVE: The learner will . . .
11.1 Be responsible for own behavior
11.2 Self-monitor own behaviors
11.3 Change own behavior as necessary
11.4 Identify and change potentially disruptive behaviors in an independent manner
11.5 Identify behaviors that interfere with own learning
11.6 Demonstrate an understanding of the importance of self-management

Standard 12. Improve organizational abilities
OBJECTIVE: The learner will . . .
12.1 Manage multiple tasks successfully
12.2 Monitor own organization of tasks
12.3 Effectively use two or more study skills to better organize task completion
12.4 Demonstrate an understanding of the importance of good organization
12.5 Begin and complete multiple tasks in a timely manner
12.6 Meet established proficiency levels by completing tasks in an organized manner
12.7 Prioritize task order to complete multiple assignments in proper sequence

for including or excluding particular goals in a study skills program must be based on many different factors, including but not limited to the following:

- Learners' educational strengths and weaknesses

- Skill areas requiring special attention

- Levels within which students are functioning relative to the skill areas requiring attention

- Students' abilities to employ the process associated with the different strategies

- School and district policies concerning teaching study skills

Information pertaining to student needs and abilities may be gathered through a variety of sources, including informal teacher assessment, teacher–student interviews, and classroom observations.

Guideline 2: Select study strategies to accommodate individual needs and abilities. Once program goals have been identified along with student strengths and weaknesses, the teacher must ensure that proper selection and effective use of the strategies occur. Although each of the student study skill strategies discussed in this book follows specific processes, teacher judgment must guide student selection and use of the different strategies. As the process associated with specific strategies is considered along with student abilities, particular study strategies may emerge as especially appropriate for different students. The teacher can ensure greater success with a study skills program by considering student abilities relative to different study strategies prior to selecting and using a particular strategy.

Guideline 3: Know what motivates your students and select study strategies accordingly. Students vary in the ways in which educational tasks motivate them. Motivation may be intrinsic (i.e., come from within the student) or extrinsic (i.e., come from external factors such as rewards or incentives). Although intrinsic motivation is preferred and necessary for productive and independent living, the extrinsic variety may be necessary to encourage some learners to engage in the use of various study skill strategies. Use of extrinsic motivators relative to study skills usage may help students to

- learn the process associated with each study skill,
- learn the proper use of each study skill strategy,
- complete assigned tasks more easily, and
- experience greater success through effective and efficient completion of daily activities.

Adhering to this guideline will help learners complete the immediate task as well as future ones more successfully as students become increasingly proficient in the use of different student study skill strategies.

Guideline 4: Demonstrate and explain to students the proper use of each study skill strategy. The concept that students must be taught when and how to use different study skill strategies is emphasized throughout this book. Through direct instruction and guided practice, students gradually and systematically acquire the process associated with each study strategy. Although the amount of time and practice required to ensure mastery of the strategies will vary from student to student, an important initial element in any study skills program is the strategic introduction, demonstration, and guided practice of various study skill strategies.

Guideline 5: Provide opportunity for continued practice and use of acquired study skills. Once students have acquired a particular study strategy and are able to employ it successfully on a regular basis, the teacher must ensure that

- learning situations exist within the classroom and other settings whereby students may employ study strategies appropriately,
- learners use different study skills strategies at appropriate times in the classroom, and
- students follow the correct procedures or processes associated with the strategies they employ.

Through careful monitoring of student use of study strategies, the teacher can best determine whether additional direct instruction is necessary or whether the learners continue to exhibit mastery of the employed study skill strategies.

Guideline 6: Informally assess response to study skills instruction. Once students are regularly applying various study strategies to address their different study skills needs, ongoing classroom-based assessment should occur to determine the impact of the study strategy usage on student learning. Form 4.2 provides a rubric to use in conjunction with other informal assessment measures to monitor student use of study skills and their application in the classroom.

Students at any grade level often require direct instruction and teacher guidance in many study skills areas, such as how to confront new vocabulary, read an assignment, take notes, write reports, take tests, manage time, or listen effectively. The six guidelines for implementing and evaluating a study skills program will assist educators in selecting strategies and teaching them to special learners in a meaningful and relevant manner. This effort may help these learners successfully confront a variety of educational tasks associated with listening, speaking, reading, writing, and thinking.

Teaching Study Skills Through Cooperative Learning

The study skills strategies, suggestions, and activities discussed in this book reflect the many ways in which students may successfully acquire and maintain study skills throughout their schooling. Helping students to address the different learning components while using their study skills facilitates the integrated learning of these skills essential for long-term retention. One current teaching practice that advocates the integration of learning through a variety of techniques is cooperative learning (Johnson & Johnson, 1998; Kagan, 1997; Slavin, 1991). Johnson and Johnson (1998) define *cooperative learning* as instructional use of small groups so that students work together to maximize learning. This type of learning contrasts with competitive and highly individualistic learning. Although competition and individualistic learning are part of cooperative learning, these forms of learning are achieved and become effective through cooperative efforts (Johnson & Johnson, 1998). Cooperative learning teams may include a small group of students or just a pair working together. In many situations (e.g., inclusive education) where students with learning problems are educated, the use of pairs may represent the best initial structure. Regardless of whether students work in pairs or in small groups, the principles of cooperative learning can be incorporated easily into the classroom (Polloway, Patton, & Serna, 2004).

As students engage in cooperative learning, the inclusion of study skills development concurrent with academic and social skills development is highly compatible with the integrated learning approach to study skills (as opposed to the isolated work on study skills for brief periods of time throughout an academic school year). Cooperative learning and its principles represent a classroom structure that may also include learning essential study skills. Whether to use cooperative learning on a regular basis in the classroom is a decision left to each individual teacher; however, if cooperative learning is used in a student's education, study skills education should be an integral part of his or her academic and social growth.

Essential Elements of Cooperative Learning

Although different researchers have identified different variations of implementing cooperative learning, five common elements are frequently discussed (Hoover & Patton, 2005; Polloway et al., 2004; Roy, 1990):

- Positive interdependence
- Individual accountability
- Provision of interactions
- Interpersonal training
- Group processing

Within the context of cooperative learning, students perceive that their goals are achieved through shared work with other students. The five listed elements facilitate this shared work, whether in the area of study skills development or in any content area (Johnson & Johnson, 1998; Roy, 1990). Each is briefly summarized in the following paragraphs.

Positive interdependence occurs when each student in the cooperative group or pair feels a sense of mutual goals and rewards. Each student understands that all members must complete the assigned tasks for the group's work to be complete. Students learn the material or task themselves and assist others in acquiring the information.

Individual accountability reflects the commitment to ensuring that each member demonstrates mastery of the assigned task, skill, or content. Each student's and the learning team's mastery levels are assessed. Cooperative learning does not exclude or excuse individuals from participating or from acquiring the material; rather, it is a structure designed to tap the strengths of each group member to facilitate learning the task or skill.

Provision of interactions is the element in which students are encouraged to assist others in learning the material. This process includes exchanging ideas, providing feedback, encouraging student efforts, discussing concepts and skills, and supporting one another's involvement. This positive and constructive interaction not only helps those being provided assistance but also offers a valuable learning experience for those helping other students. Although the quantity and quality of these types of student interactions will vary, regular practice in facilitating student assistance and interactions strengthens the sharing of information in a cooperative manner.

Interpersonal training involves preparing students for successful interactions in cooperative learning teams. Teachers must help students with communication, conflict management, decision making, leadership, and other related group-oriented interaction skills. Students with special learning needs may require assistance and encouragement in this area. Groups of two or three students, some of whom possess these skills, allow individuals the opportunity to share their skills with others, supported by teacher intervention. The success of small cooperative groups relies heavily on proper student preparation by the teacher in how the teams should function. In many situations, the direct teaching of specific study skills (e.g., self-management of behavior, notetaking and outlining, time management) will facilitate this student preparation.

Group processing provides students and teachers the opportunity to determine how well the pair or group functioned relative to specific tasks. Cooperative team members discuss individual contributions to the group, ways to improve overall member interactions and contributions, and recommendations for future cooperative team efforts. Use of a student or teacher observer of the group's activities may facilitate processing the group's interactions.

Implementing Cooperative Learning

A cooperative learning environment in the classroom requires emphasis on each of the five elements described in the previous section. Once teachers have ensured that students possess a minimum level of skills necessary for group interaction (i.e., interpersonal training), cooperative learning may begin. Although the structure of activities, lessons, room arrangements, and evaluation of performance will vary across cooperative learning groups, research in the area of this teaching practice provides evidence of its effectiveness with students. According to Slavin (1991), cooperative learning is effective in enhancing student achievement in all major subject areas in elementary and secondary grades, and for low-, average-, and high-achieving students. Slavin states further that "cooperative learning usually supplements the teacher's interaction by giving students an opportunity to discuss information or practice skills originally presented by the teacher" (p. 83).

In support, Johnson and Johnson (1998) assert that cooperative learning is effective in helping students learn basic facts, understand concepts, problem solve, and use higher level thinking skills. The learning components discussed previously that are addressed through study skills use—that is, acquisition, recording, organization, memorization, synthesis, and location—represent higher level thinking skills, as well as problem solving and concept development. Slavin (1991) found that, of the five critical elements associated with cooperative learning, individual accountability and group processing elements were the most important in the success of this approach.

Cooperative learning has been found to be helpful in the education of students with special learning needs. Johnson and Johnson (1998) report that cooperative learning strategies are effective with students with disabilities. Salend (2000) cites several researchers who support the use of cooperative learning with students who have learning problems and are placed in inclusive settings.

When implementing cooperative learning, teachers should follow several guidelines. Developed from information found in several sources, this list summarizes important factors necessary for cooperative learning to be successful (Johnson & Johnson, 1998).

- The group or pair produces one product.
- Team members assist others.
- Team members seek assistance when necessary from other team members.
- Team members discuss ideas prior to changing any previously agreed upon ideas or issues.
- Each team member accepts responsibility for the completed project or task.
- Each member participates in the group activities.
- Each member provides input into the group-processing aspect of the team's activities.
- Individual accountability for learning the task or concept prevails along with expectations of group interactions.

Cooperative learning has been found effective with a variety of students in various subject areas who possess varying skill levels. The implementation of cooperative learning may involve a variety of groupings or pairs with an emphasis on different content areas. In this text, we emphasize the ways to include study skills development within the structure of cooperative learning; for more detailed discussions about specific strategies for implementing cooperative learning, the reader is referred to Johnson and Johnson (1998). The following discussion provides examples of how teachers may address study skills development while simultaneously addressing the five essential elements for implementing cooperative learning within the guidelines outlined above.

Study Skills and Cooperative Learning

Study skills have been defined in this book as tools or support skills that students must employ to effectively and efficiently record, organize, synthesize, and evaluate tasks and skills in the overall process of learning. Previous discussion also has noted the emphasis on these and similar higher level thinking skills frequently encountered in the effective implementation of cooperative learning. As students engage in learning, regular and consistent use of study skills is necessary. Efficient use of study skills becomes even more important as tasks and concepts become more complex. As a result, whether students are working independently or in a cooperative learning group, they must develop and apply a variety of study skills to meet the demands of assigned tasks.

Table 4.2 provides an overview of how study skills development is a natural and integral part of a cooperative learning structure; the five essential elements associated with cooperative learning are directly impacted by student use of study skills. This developmental sequence includes the following features:

- Impact on the overall performance of members within the group or pair
- The identification, development, and maintenance of various study skills
- The sharing of strategies for effective use of study skills
- The importance of different study skills to the overall process of cooperative learning
- The reflection of study skills usage by group or pair members

A direct relationship exists between effective use of study skills and the efficient implementation of cooperative learning. For example, an individual's inefficient use of time, poor self-management of behavior, inappropriate library and reference material usage, poor test-taking skills, or ineffective use of reading rates will interfere with the successful learning of most tasks or content through cooperative learning. While reading the next chapter, which focuses on teaching specific study skills, the reader is advised to consider the importance of incorporating an ongoing study skills program within cooperative learning just as it should be within the various content areas and classroom structures.

Semantic Webbing and Study Skills

Using semantic webs frequently is discussed as an effective practice for assisting with reading comprehension and related areas of learning (Harris & Sipay, 1990; Polloway et al., 2004). Through semantic webbing, students relate new knowledge with existing knowledge. Teachers can use semantic webbing to help students learn and apply study skills within actual classroom situations (Hoover, 2004b).

Semantic webbing allows students to build systematically on their previous study skills knowledge and experiences, no matter how inexperienced they are with using study skills in learning (Hoover & Rabideau, 1995). Table 4.3 lists 10 of the

Table 4.2
Study Skills Development and Cooperative Learning

Cooperative Learning Elements	Study Skills Development
Positive interdependence	Effective study skills usage by each member affects, in a positive way, the actions and learning of all members within a cooperative learning group or pair.
Individual accountability	As individuals within a group recognize their own study skills strengths and weaknesses, they are able to identify ways to best contribute to the group and ways the group may best assist them with their study skills development. Pre- and postassessments of study skills abilities will ensure that individual accountability is maintained.
Provision of interactions	Once individual strengths and weaknesses in the use of study skills have been identified, students are better prepared to help others with study skills they may already possess as well as to learn from others. Exchanging study skills ideas and strategies that have been effective and are relevant to completion of the cooperative learning task at hand will serve to strengthen the study skills abilities of group members. It also will provide a basis for the constructive interactions and decision making required for effective cooperative learning to occur.
Interpersonal training	A major goal of any comprehensive study skills program is to promote greater independence in learning. As teachers engage students in interpersonal training activities, study skills should be an integral part of this training. As students become proficient with skills such as time management, self-management of behavior, notetaking, and library usage, they will be better prepared to engage in interpersonal interactions relative to a cooperative learning academic task. Interpersonal training will not be complete unless these and similar study skills are mastered.
Group processing	As students engage in discussions and reflect on how well their group or pair functioned relative to specific tasks, the specific study skills used to facilitate completion of the task or learn the content should be addressed.

most widely needed study skills along with several suggested semantic web topics for which students may generate subordinate ideas. The main topics appear in bold, with suggested subtopics in italic. As shown, many different semantic web topics or subtopics can aid learners in their study skills usage, and these may be adapted and expanded easily. Specific topics as well as procedures for using semantic webbing in the classroom will vary from teacher to teacher as student skill levels and needs are determined; however, a number of general principles should be followed to ensure its effective use in meeting the study skills needs of students with learning problems (Hoover, 2004a; Polloway et al., 2004):

1. Complete the web as a whole class, or allow students to work in small, cooperative groups of 3 to 4 members.
2. If small groups are used, assign one student in the group the task of recording responses for the group.

Table 4.3

Semantic Web Topics for Major Study Skills

Study Skill	Learning Importance	Semantic Web Topics
Reading rate	Reading rates vary with type and length of reading assignments.	**Fast-paced, slow-paced rates,** *getting main idea, locating details, determining sequence of ideas, retaining information*
Listening	Listening skills are necessary to complete most educational tasks or requirements.	**Formal lectures, small group discussions, audiovisual presentations,** *attending to message, clarifying speaker's ideas, applying meaning to message, remembering message*
Library usage	Library usage skills facilitate easy access to much information.	**Cataloguing system, library organization, media specialist role**
Reference materials	Independent learning may be greatly improved through effective use of reference materials and dictionaries.	**Dictionary, encyclopedia, atlas, Internet,** *material's purpose, finding information, guide words, table of contents, glossary*
Test taking	Effective test-taking abilities help ensure more accurate assessment of student abilities.	**Essay tests, multiple-choice tests, short answer tests,** *studying for tests, taking the test, reviewing the completed test*
Notetaking and outlining	Effective notetaking and outlining skills allow students to document key points of topics for future study.	**Formal papers, draft papers, research projects,** *organizing notes, sufficient details, headings and subheadings, organizational format, collecting ideas*
Oral presentations	Students must use various methods for presenting information effectively.	**Written reports, oral presentations, visual presentations,** *topic selection, organizing thoughts, proper grammar, punctuation, using visuals, speaking mechanics*
Time management	Time management assists in reducing the number of unfinished assignments and facilitates more effective use of time.	**Task identification, prioritizing tasks, recording task completion, daily, weekly, and monthly schedules**
Self-management	Self-management assists students in assuming responsibility for their own behaviors.	**Monitoring own behavior, assuming responsibility, changing own behavior**
Organization	Organizational abilities assist students to manage multiple tasks.	**Managing multiple tasks, prioritizing work, demonstrating understanding of effective organization**

3. Present the students with a main study skill topic for the semantic web (e.g., test taking, listening, report writing, time management), as well as important subtopics, if necessary.
4. Engage students in a brainstorming session to generate key subordinate words or phrases they believe relate to or describe the main study skill or subtopics (write these within the web as generated by the students).

5. Once completed, discuss with the students how specific subordinate items can be used to further develop use of the study skill.
6. Students should apply selected elements of their choice from their study skill semantic webs to further develop their acquisition, maintenance, and generalization of the study skills. Monitor this process on an ongoing basis.
7. Initially, students should work with only one web at a time. Once they are familiar with this process of learning, introduce additional webs as needed.
8. Each student should refer to the completed web to help him or her use and learn the study skill. This process should occur for an extended period of time to ensure generalization and overlearning.
9. Students should compile and keep all of their study skills semantic webs in a notebook for easy reference and future use.

As students engage in the semantic webbing process, prior knowledge of their use of the study skill is activated. In sharing this prior knowledge with others, they add new information to each student's experiences concerning the study skill. This process allows students to see how others use the same study skills as well as the various reasons why the study skill is an important learning tool. Semantic webbing also helps students see potential problems that others have encountered in using the study skill, as well as ways to confront these potential problems effectively.

To assist students in the actual development of a semantic web, teachers should consider the following suggestions:

- Explain to students that they will employ a webbing strategy to explore different study skills they have been using (or will use) and to organize this information for future application.

- Assist students in developing a skeleton semantic web or provide one to them.

- Prior to actual web development, ask students to share specific examples of where they use the study skill and then list these on the board (e.g., reference materials are used during library time, to complete independent projects, to understand word meanings, and to supplement information studied).

- When using cooperative work groups, assign a recorder of ideas and discuss the importance of sharing within the group.

- As students brainstorm key subordinate words or phrases associated with the main study skill or subtopics, they may refer to the list of examples to trigger additional ideas.

- Encourage all students to share in the semantic web, emphasizing the importance of each contribution.

- After the web has been completed and discussed, provide each student with a copy of the completed version for future use.

Semantic Web: Test-Taking Example

Figure 4.2 provides an example of a semantic web for helping students complete multiple-choice tests. In this example, the teacher identifies the main topic (Test Taking: Multiple Choice) and the related subtopics (studying for the test, taking the test, reviewing the completed test). The items surrounding the subtopics are examples of student-generated ideas for using the study skill and for applying the subtopics to their test taking. Once the web has been completed by a pair or a small group of students, each learner should receive a copy and select

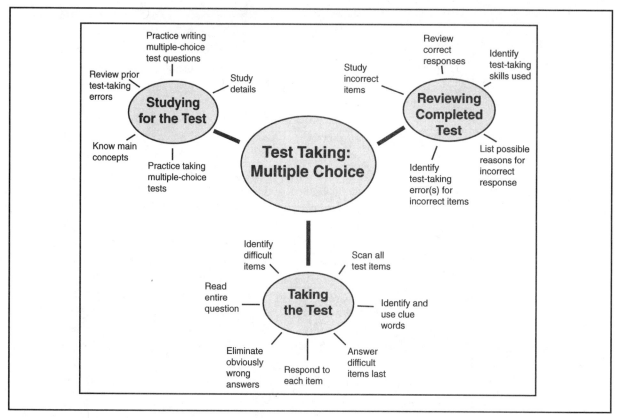

Figure 4.2. Semantic web of the "Test Taking: Multiple Choice" study skill. *Note.* From "Semantic Webs and Study Skills," by J. J. Hoover and D. K. Rabideau, 1995, *Intervention in School and Clinic, 30,* p. 295. Copyright 1995 by PRO-ED, Inc. Reprinted with permission.

one or two ideas from it to begin to apply in his or her learning. After students complete a multiple-choice test, they should analyze why and in what ways the web ideas helped them and what they can do in the future to best study for, complete, and review their multiple-choice tests.

Semantic Web: Time Management Example

Figure 4.3 illustrates a semantic web for the study skill of time management. In this example, only a main topic is addressed along with subordinate ideas. Students should initially provide examples of where time management is useful and important in learning. These statements should be listed on the board and referred to as the various subordinate ideas are generated.

Once the whole class or small groups have completed the web, the whole group should discuss ways to implement the subordinate ideas, referring to the list of examples that describe where time management is used. Teachers should assist students in developing their own daily, weekly, and/or monthly schedules using the subordinate ideas. In addition, teachers should make certain that students have a procedure for documenting completion of tasks and allow them to review their time management schedules daily. By meeting in pairs or small groups to discuss progress in meeting time management schedules, students are able to share and learn how others addressed similar tasks. Educators may need to hold individual conferences with students concerning their time management and selected semantic web ideas or may choose to follow other procedures described in the previous semantic web example. Specifically, teachers should help students

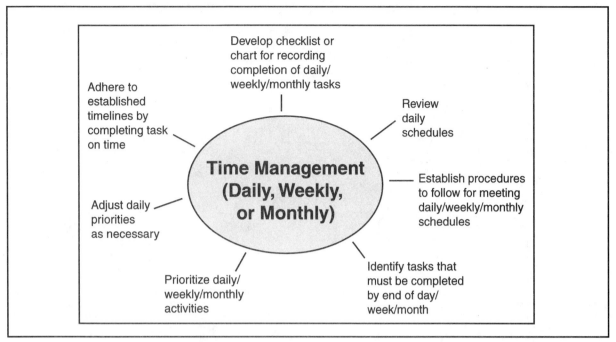

Figure 4.3. Semantic web of the "Time Management" study skill. *Note.* From "Semantic Webs and Study Skills," by J. J. Hoover and D. K. Rabideau, 1995, *Intervention in School and Clinic, 30,* p. 295. Copyright 1995 by PRO-ED, Inc. Reprinted with permission.

select and apply the semantic web subordinate ideas in their time management at school and home. Also, if necessary, students can complete individual semantic webs for each type of time management schedule (i.e., daily, weekly, monthly), even though similar subordinate ideas may be generated.

Follow-up to Semantic Webbing

Teachers should encourage the students to add more information to their study skills semantic webs as they continue in their application and development of the study skills. Students will need teacher guidance on how to apply their semantic webs to classroom tasks. Although the process of completing the web constitutes a major part of the learning, regular application of the semantic web information in learning will ensure continued growth in the use of specific study skills.

Students with learning difficulties may require specific training or coaching to successfully complete semantic webbing in a cooperative work group. Teachers must consider individual student needs to determine the extent of each student's involvement in the process. However, the more students are able to share study skill experiences with each other, the more they see that others experience similar successes and problems with the same study skill. This sharing serves to improve confidence in use of the study skill and greater understanding of its classroom application. Therefore, a critical follow-up component in the use of semantic webbing in developing and using study skills is the application of what is learned during web completion and follow-up discussions to actual learning situations where the study skill must be used to successfully complete learning tasks (Hoover, 2004b).

FORM 4.1

Study Skills Inventory

Student Name _____ Grade _____

Completed by _____ Date _____

Directions: Rate each item using the scale provided. Base the rating on the individual's present level of performance.

Study Skill	Rating			
	Not Proficient	Partially Proficient	Proficient	Highly Proficient
Reading Rate				
Skims	0	1	2	3
Scans	0	1	2	3
Reads at rapid rate	0	1	2	3
Reads at normal rate	0	1	2	3
Reads at study or careful rate	0	1	2	3
Understands the importance of reading	0	1	2	3
Listening				
Attends to listening activities	0	1	2	3
Applies meaning to verbal messages	0	1	2	3
Filters out auditory distractions	0	1	2	3
Comprehends verbal messages	0	1	2	3
Understands importance of listening skills	0	1	2	3
Graphic Aids				
Attends to relevant elements in visual material	0	1	2	3
Uses visuals appropriately in presentations	0	1	2	3
Develops own graphic material	0	1	2	3
Is not confused or distracted by visual material in presentations	0	1	2	3
Understands importance of visual material	0	1	2	3
Library Usage				
Uses cataloging system (card or computerized) effectively	0	1	2	3
Can locate library materials	0	1	2	3

(continues)

Study Skills Inventory

Study Skill	Rating			
	Not Proficient	Partially Proficient	Proficient	Highly Proficient
Library Usage (*continued*)				
Understands organizational layout of library	0	1	2	3
Understands and uses services of media specialist	0	1	2	3
Understands overall functions and purposes of a library	0	1	2	3
Understands importance of library usage skills	0	1	2	3
Reference Materials				
Can identify components of different reference materials	0	1	2	3
Uses guide words appropriately	0	1	2	3
Consults reference materials when necessary	0	1	2	3
Uses materials appropriately to complete assignments	0	1	2	3
Can identify different types of reference materials and sources	0	1	2	3
Understands importance of reference materials	0	1	2	3
Test Taking				
Studies for tests in an organized way	0	1	2	3
Spends appropriate amount of time studying different topics covered on a test	0	1	2	3
Avoids cramming for tests	0	1	2	3
Organizes narrative responses appropriately	0	1	2	3
Reads and understands directions before answering questions	0	1	2	3
Proofreads responses and checks for errors	0	1	2	3
Identifies and uses clue words in questions	0	1	2	3
Properly records answers	0	1	2	3
Saves difficult items until last	0	1	2	3
Eliminates obvious wrong answers	0	1	2	3
Systematically reviews completed tests to determine test-taking or test-studying errors	0	1	2	3
Corrects previous test-taking errors	0	1	2	3
Understands importance of test-taking skills	0	1	2	3

(continues)

FORM 4.1 *Continued.*

Study Skills Inventory

Study Skill	Rating			
	Not Proficient	Partially Proficient	Proficient	Highly Proficient
Notetaking and Outlining				
Uses headings (and subheadings) appropriately	0	1	2	3
Takes brief and clear notes	0	1	2	3
Records essential information	0	1	2	3
Applies skill during writing activities	0	1	2	3
Uses skill during lectures	0	1	2	3
Develops organized outlines	0	1	2	3
Follows consistent notetaking format	0	1	2	3
Understands importance of notetaking	0	1	2	3
Understands importance of outlining	0	1	2	3
Report Writing				
Organizes thoughts in writing	0	1	2	3
Completes written reports from outline	0	1	2	3
Includes only necessary information	0	1	2	3
Uses proper sentence structure	0	1	2	3
Uses proper punctuation	0	1	2	3
Uses proper grammar and spelling	0	1	2	3
Proofreads written assignments	0	1	2	3
Provides clear introductory statement	0	1	2	3
Includes clear concluding statements	0	1	2	3
Understands importance of writing reports	0	1	2	3
Oral Presentations				
Freely participates in oral presentations	0	1	2	3
Organizes presentations well	0	1	2	3
Uses gestures appropriately	0	1	2	3
Speaks clearly	0	1	2	3
Uses proper language when reporting orally	0	1	2	3

(continues)

Study Skills Inventory

Study Skill	Rating			
	Not Proficient	Partially Proficient	Proficient	Highly Proficient
Oral Presentations *(continued)*				
Understands importance of oral reporting	0	1	2	3
Time Management				
Completes tasks on time	0	1	2	3
Plans and organizes daily activities and responsibilities effectively	0	1	2	3
Plans and organizes weekly and monthly schedules	0	1	2	3
Reorganizes priorities when necessary	0	1	2	3
Meets scheduled deadlines	0	1	2	3
Accurately perceives the amount of time required to complete tasks	0	1	2	3
Adjusts time allotment to complete tasks	0	1	2	3
Accepts responsibility for managing own time	0	1	2	3
Understands importance of effective time management	0	1	2	3
Self-Management				
Monitors own behavior	0	1	2	3
Changes own behavior as necessary	0	1	2	3
Thinks before acting	0	1	2	3
Is responsible for own behavior	0	1	2	3
Identifies behaviors that interfere with own learning	0	1	2	3
Understands importance of self-management	0	1	2	3
Organization				
Uses locker efficiently	0	1	2	3
Transports books and other material to and from school effectively	0	1	2	3
Has books, supplies, equipment, and other materials needed for class	0	1	2	3
Manages multiple tasks or assignments	0	1	2	3
Uses two or more study skills simultaneously when needed	0	1	2	3
Meets individual organizational expectations concerning own learning	0	1	2	3

(continues)

FORM 4.1 *Continued.*

Summary of Study Skills Performance

Directions: Summarize in the chart below the number of Not Proficient (NP), Partially Proficient (PP), Proficient (P), and Highly Proficient (HP) subskills for each study skill. The number next to the study skill represents the total number of subskills listed for each area.

Study Skill	NP	PP	P	HP
Reading rate (6)				
Listening (5)				
Graphic aids (5)				
Library usage (6)				
Reference materials (6)				
Test taking (13)				

Study Skill	NP	PP	P	HP
Notetaking and outlining (9)				
Report writing (10)				
Oral presentations (6)				
Time management (9)				
Self-management (6)				
Organization (6)				

Summary comments about student study skills:

_____

_____

_____

_____

_____

_____

_____

Rubric for Evaluating Impact of Study Skills Usage

Directions: Circle the level of usage for each specific study skill.

Student Name _____

Study Skill	1 Minimal usage of skill/ No impact on learning	2 Some usage/Irregular impact on learning	3 Consistent usage/Regular impact on most learning	4 Daily usage/Noticeable impact on most daily learning
Reading rate	1	2	3	4
Listening	1	2	3	4
Graphic aids	1	2	3	4
Library usage	1	2	3	4
Reference materials	1	2	3	4
Test taking	1	2	3	4
Notetaking and outlining	1	2	3	4
Report writing	1	2	3	4
Oral presentations	1	2	3	4
Time management	1	2	3	4
Self-management	1	2	3	4
Organization	1	2	3	4

Comments: _____

_____

_____

5

Teaching Study Skills

An effectively managed study skills program includes student uses of a variety of study and learning strategies to meet diverse educational needs in the classroom.

This chapter provides a more detailed discussion of the 12 study skills introduced in the previous chapters. The study skills fit into the three standards-based groupings: content, performance, and opportunities to learn. To support study skills instruction, the appendix includes a guide for identifying problems in using each study skill area, along with numerous guides and checklists for student and teacher use. Guides for student use may be completed individually by students or cooperatively with teachers. Each study skill discussion includes numerous teaching strategies to assist students in developing use of the skill.

Content Standards

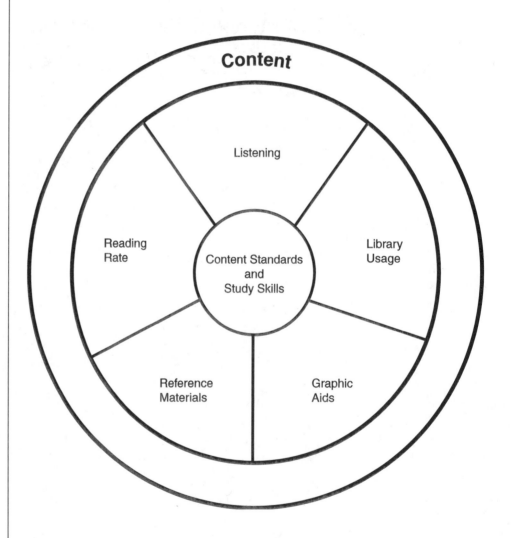

Reading Rate: Key to Reading Success

The critical elements of this study skill are knowing when to use

- Fast-paced rates (skimming, scanning, rapid reading)
- Slow-paced rates (normal reading, study-type reading)

Importance of Reading Rate in School

Reading is a crucial area of learning that permeates all or most educational tasks. Efficient readers vary their rates of reading when completing assigned tasks. The particular rate of reading appropriate to any reading assignment is determined by the nature of the material and the overall purpose for reading it. Students have many purposes for reading, including the following:

- To review information
- To get the main idea
- To find a specific name or event in a story
- To answer detailed questions
- To master specific content
- To memorize information
- To evaluate topics or issues
- To study for tests

In addition, students may read for recreational purposes or work-related reasons.

The purpose for reading and the type of reading material require decisions related to reading rate. For example, rates for reading highly technical information, poetry, recipes, math word problems, or computer software vary from person to person depending on the purposes for reading the material and the reader's proficiency level with these types of materials. The inability to use different reading rates may inhibit students from completing assigned tasks on time because (a) extended periods of time are required to read the material or (b) interference with comprehension may result from inappropriately paced reading. The flexible use of reading rates helps students to complete a variety of assignments both efficiently and effectively.

Elements Related to Reading Rates

Various reading rates are typically required of students to complete required tasks in different subject areas. These rates may be summarized as follows:

Fast-Paced Rates
Skimming

Scanning

Rapid reading

Slow-Paced Rates
Normal reading

Study-type reading

Fast-paced reading rates allow students to find general answers or ideas in reading material as well as to identify specific items in a timely and efficient manner. Careful reading rates allow students to master details, memorize information, and engage in reading-related tasks requiring more complex analysis and comprehension of reading material. Each of these is described in more detail below.

Another way to conceptualize the use of various reading rates is based on why the technique is needed and how reading material is to be used. The various rates serve different functions, as depicted in Figure 5.1. As can be seen from the figure, techniques such as skimming and scanning serve a short-term need and provide a cursory understanding of the material read; the normal and study-type reading rates address long-term needs and provide a more detailed understanding of the material.

Skimming is a fast-paced rate of reading used to grasp general ideas. When skimming, the reader can glance through portions of the reading material to obtain a general idea of its content. A reader may use skimming to obtain an overview of a chapter in a book before beginning more detailed reading, to review several pages (such as of a story) to form an overall impression and decide whether to read the entire piece, to quickly review material to determine if it contains specific information the reader is seeking, or to determine if the general reading level of the material is too easy or difficult for the reader. Skimming helps students select and use reading material that is specific and appropriate to a stated purpose. It also helps students to reduce time wasted by reading material that is not specific to the task at hand.

Scanning is a fast-paced rate of reading that is applied when the reader is searching for a specific item or piece of information. When the reader needs to find, for example, a name, telephone number, date, or event in a story, scanning often serves. The effective use of scanning allows students to review material rapidly and to determine quickly whether they have reached the part of the story or material they are seeking. It also allows students to focus specifically on the item in question when they encounter it in the selection. The proficient scanner can achieve great speed reviewing material in search of specific items.

Rapid reading, a third type of fast-paced reading, serves when the reader wishes to grasp, in general, the main idea of a story. Specific purposes for the rapid reading rate include (a) obtaining information that will be used on a temporary basis, (b) rereading familiar material, (c) ascertaining the general plot of a selection, or (d) obtaining ideas for purely informational and recreational purposes. Similar to skimming and scanning, rapid reading allows the reader to review material quickly for both work-related and recreational tasks.

The *normal rate of reading* applies for a variety of complex tasks, such as identifying specific details that are more comprehensive than those found using scanning procedures, solving problems, grasping relationships among details and story ideas, or reading material of average difficulty to the reader. The normal reading rate is used frequently in school as students attempt many daily instructional tasks. It may also be employed for various recreational purposes or when the reader desires sufficient information to share the contents of the material with others at a later time. This rate of reading is used for many reading tasks when more than a cursory overview of the material is desired.

The *study-type reading rate,* an extension of the normal reading rate, is applied when students must master significant details, evaluate reading material, analyze an author's position or presentation, solve problems in greater detail, or read a unique

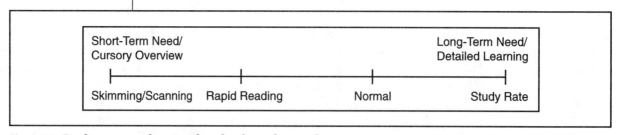

Figure 5.1. Reading rate as a function of need and use of material.

vocabulary and writing style as is sometimes found in poetry or technical material. Study-type reading is often required to memorize material and to follow specific, detailed directions.

These five different rates of reading enable students to address various types of reading assignments for various purposes. Reading rates become very important as students engage in reading for comprehension, whether at a simple or a complex level of difficulty.

Identifying Reading-Rate Needs

The Guide for Identifying Reading-Rate Needs (Form 5.1) offers a springboard for identifying potential problems associated with reading rates. These and similar indicators of potential problems address the reader's inability to exercise flexibility in the use of reading rates. As teachers work with and observe students engaged in different reading tasks, they should focus on the students' ability to vary their reading rates. In addition, teachers should determine whether and in what types of reading tasks students use skimming, scanning, rapid reading, normal reading, and study-type reading.

Students who spend unusually long periods of time completing reading tasks that typically should take brief amounts of time may be inappropriately using a slow-paced reading rate. Although the correct response or end result often occurs, the learners have spent time engaged in a reading task that could have been spent on other activities if a faster rate had been used. These situations take time away not only from other school-related tasks but also from recreational activities.

Conversely, students who spend unusually short periods of time completing tasks that require more detailed study often are using a fast-paced reading rate when a careful one is required. In these situations, overall reading comprehension and mastery of details may suffer. Some students may grasp a portion of the material necessary to complete the assignment or take a test; however, they may not acquire other portions of the material and therefore receive lower grades or do not finish assignments. Whether students read to complete homework, to study for a test, to review daily class notes, or for general recreation and enjoyment, they must apply reading rates appropriately.

Effective use of fast-paced reading rates (skimming, scanning, and rapid reading) and careful reading rates (normal and study-type rates) provides students the best opportunity to complete reading-related tasks efficiently and effectively. Inability to vary reading rates contributes to unfinished assignments, superficial completion of assignments, only cursory knowledge of course content, or less than adequate preparation for tests and other major educational tasks.

The flexible use of reading rates contributes to more effective studying in any content area and allows students a greater opportunity to constructively use their time before, during, and after studying activities. If an individual does not currently vary reading rates for different types of reading tasks and material, the student needs to learn to adjust reading rates appropriately.

Reading Rate: Best Practices

- Instruct students to examine reading material to determine approximate difficulty level prior to reading the material (Harris & Sipay, 1990).
- Provide students with several written sentences from a passage, omitting selected key words. Instruct the students to complete the sentences after

reading the passage using different reading rates. Discuss the effects of different rates on the ability to complete the missing words.

- Instruct students to scan several paragraphs to find the name of a specific person, and then ask them for a specific detail at that point in the story.

- Review the index for selected topics, and have students identify the page numbers where these topics are discussed.

- Encourage students to select a reading passage and generate questions that require use of different reading rates to obtain the answers.

- After presenting new words to students, instruct them to scan the story to find the first time each word is used.

- Alternate the need to use different types of reading rates in the same material by requesting answers to general and significant details.

- Ensure that proper reading rates are used for different types of activities.

- Establish clear purposes for reading assignments.

- Ensure that each student understands when and how to use each type of reading rate.

- Encourage students to reread sections of material when comprehension is poor, emphasizing the proper reading rate.

- Provide opportunities for practicing each reading rate.

Guide for Identifying Reading-Rate Needs

Student Name _____

Completed by _____ Date _____

Directions: Check the box next to each behavior that the student exhibits on a regular and consistent basis. Summarize the areas of need to complete the guide.

☐ Takes an unusually long amount of time to find specific names or events in a story

☐ Reads an unusually large portion of a story or book before realizing that the material is too difficult for him or her

☐ Reads unfamiliar material too quickly when the overall purpose is to master details and memorize information

☐ Takes an unusually long amount of time to review previously read and learned material

☐ Has a difficult time previewing material to determine its general content

☐ Reads, at a slow pace, an extended amount of a selection before realizing that the material does not contain the information that he or she must find

☐ Uses fast-paced reading rates when the normal or study-type rate is required

☐ Reads unfamiliar and highly technical information at the same rate used for reviewing familiar material.

☐ Is unable to discuss the uses of various reading rates after apparently using the different rates for an extended period of time

☐ Uses careful, slower paced rates of reading to complete activities that can be completed easily and accurately using one or more of the fast-paced rates of reading

Summary comments: _____

_____

_____

_____

Listening: Comprehending Verbal Communication

The critical elements of this study skill are

- Attending to listening tasks
- Applying meaning to verbal messages
- Filtering out auditory distractions

Importance of Listening in School

Approximately two thirds of a learner's school day is spent in listening-related tasks or activities. Much of what occurs at school relies heavily on one's ability to listen. Listening involves the complex processes associated with hearing, memory storage, and recall, as well as critical thinking to determine primary and secondary importance associated with what is heard. Many students, however, do not remember much of what they "listen to" even if they presumably heard the message in the first place.

Although educators continually discuss the importance of supplementing listening activities with visual aids or hands-on experiences to increase retention, students must learn to listen. Some of the more crucial reasons for listening include (a) taking notes during lecture situations, (b) understanding particular expectations during different types of learning situations, (c) following directions, and (d) following a sequence of events or ideas. Learning through listening is therefore fundamental to the most basic school activities and is a study skill that learners must develop and practice to complete school successfully.

Elements Related to Listening

To demonstrate effective listening, students must be able to

- receive the information,
- apply meaning to what is heard, and
- provide some evidence of understanding what is heard.

These three elements of listening emphasize the importance of both hearing and comprehending a verbal message. In any particular listening situation, students may (a) not hear the message, (b) hear the message but not comprehend what is heard, or (c) hear and comprehend the message. *Hearing* refers to receiving the information, whereas *comprehending* indicates that meaning has been applied to what was heard. Students may show that they have comprehended a verbal message in a variety of ways, including following directions, taking notes, paraphrasing, outlining and summarizing, or applying what was heard to new situations.

Identifying Listening Needs

The Guide for Identifying Listening Needs (Form 5.2) can be used to identify potential problems associated with effective listening. The listed indicators represent some of the problems poor listeners may exhibit. Because listening is required at home as well as in school, teachers should determine whether some of these indicators are evident at home when verbal interactions occur. Students with good listening skills are able to filter out various distractions, understand the difference between primary and secondary points in an oral message, follow oral directions on a regular basis, and in general acquire necessary information to complete tasks through a variety of listening activities at school. Because the development of good listening skills requires practice, efforts at school can increase the learner's ability to listen more effectively.

Effective listening is essential for the successful completion of school and for the overall development of independent living skills. Ensuring that students hear and comprehend spoken messages is important to the development of good listening. By expecting students to attend to and concentrate on oral information, teachers can help them learn how to listen, which will contribute to the continued development and application of effective listening at school. When problems associated with listening are apparent, learners' physical ability to hear should be checked. If examination determines no hearing problem yet difficulties with listening activities persist, more specific investigation into potential listening problems should be undertaken. Some indicators of potential listening problems are addressed on Form 5.2.

Listening: Best Practices

- Minimize distractions and quickly deal with disruptions.
- Ensure that all students are located in the classroom so they are able to hear.
- Encourage students to speak loudly enough that all can hear.
- Repeat important items and emphasize important content in the verbal message.
- Begin lectures at a point familiar to all students and gradually bridge to new material.
- Assist students in realizing the importance of the material being presented.
- Provide frequent summaries at strategic points in the verbal message.
- Prior to lecturing, write an outline of the lecture on the board. At strategic points in the lecture, stop and ask students to identify the next point to be discussed on the outline.
- Upon completion of a lecture, instruct students to outline the important points.
- At strategic points in a lecture, ask students to summarize the material just presented and to predict the next topic to be covered.
- Instruct students to identify all sounds they hear during a specified time period. Discuss potential problems that may arise if these sounds occur during a lecture.
- Instruct students to listen for special sequencing words or phrases (e.g., *first, second, in summary*) (Wallace & Kauffman, 1990).
- Instruct one student to interview a second student about a specific topic while a third student observes the interview. Upon completion of the interview, ask each to summarize what was said and then compare interpretations of the interview.
- Ask students to paraphrase directions for various assignments (e.g., homework, independent work, a spelling assignment).

- Instruct students to generate a list of "good listener" guidelines (e.g., looking at the person speaking, remaining quiet) and post it strategically in the room.

- At the start of a lecture, inform students that one or more factual errors exist in the lecture. Instruct them to identify the error(s) upon completion of the lecture.

- Prior to a lecture, list on the board several questions that are addressed in the lecture. Discuss the questions after completing the lecture.

- Prior to a lecture, list its most important topics on the board, out of sequence. Instruct the students to arrange the topics in the correct order following the lecture.

Guide for Identifying Listening Needs

Student Name _____

Completed by _____ Date _____

Directions: Check the box next to each behavior that the student exhibits on a regular and consistent basis. Summarize the areas of need to complete the guide.

☐ Is unable to concentrate during listening activities

☐ Frequently loses attention due to visual distractions during listening activities

☐ Frequently loses attention due to auditory distractions during listening activities

☐ Is unable to identify primary and secondary points in a verbal message

☐ Is unable to follow verbal directions when repeated several times

☐ Appears to attend to the speaker but is unable to summarize what the person said

☐ Is unable to interpret and evaluate a verbal message even though facts from the message are learned

☐ Is unable to anticipate what may come next in a verbal message after listening to a substantial portion of the message

☐ Is unable to state purposes of a listening activity

☐ Exhibits boredom or an uninterested attitude toward listening activities

☐ Demonstrates overall inability to learn content or skills when taught primarily through listening activities

Summary comments: _____

_____

_____

_____

Graphic Aids: Understanding Visual Material

The critical elements of this study skill are

- Understanding the purposes of graphic aids
- Developing one's own graphic aids
- Attending to the relevant elements of graphic aids

Importance of Graphic Aids in School

Much of the reading material found in school contains visual aids in the form of pictures, graphs, tables, figures, or assorted diagrams. Graphic material has various uses in school, including the following:

- Presentation of complex material in visual form facilitates greater comprehension of that material.

- Graphic illustrations may present large abstractions in small, visual, and manageable pieces.

- Differences and similarities among cultural, economic, or geographic situations may be effectively depicted and studied in visual-aid form.

- Visual material often provides a good summary of a topic discussed in several pages of text.

- Graphic materials often assist in the explanation of a variety of topics or issues found in written reports, oral presentations, textbook readings, or lectures.

In addition, the viewing, developing, and studying of graphic aids require students to think about what they see and apply or connect it to what they are reading or hearing. As a result, graphic aids require the use of thinking skills along with listening or reading abilities. Graphic aids may be either essential or supplemental to the learning task as students attempt to grasp the complete meaning of a topic or skill. Unfortunately, too often students skim over visual aids and miss important presentations of information.

Elements of Graphic Aids

Although graphic aids may take many forms and be displayed in a variety of ways, they are developed solely to provide a clear and accurate depiction of a topic. When interpreting graphic aids, students should systematically study the elements found in the visuals as follows:

- Read the titles or captions associated with the visual.
- Survey the entire visual initially to grasp its overall meaning.
- Identify the reason for its inclusion in the printed material or verbal presentation.
- Draw conclusions related to information obtained from the visual material.

Visual material may also include different units of measurement, representing perhaps a scale model; proportions; numbers of days, weeks, or years; or percentages. Students must initially identify any units of measurement used in visual material and be certain they understand what the units mean. Not understanding various units of measurement makes reading graphs, diagrams, tables, or figures very difficult, if not impossible.

Whether the graphic aid is a picture illustrating a concept, a chart or table summarizing data, or a physical object used in an oral presentation, the elements within the visual aid must be identified and understood and related to the context in which it is presented. Students must put forth effort to study and interpret each element of the graphic aid; otherwise, it may become just another page in a book or display in a presentation, and a good opportunity to more fully grasp a concept or idea becomes lost.

Identifying Graphic Aids Needs

Students with well-developed abilities in using graphic aids are able to attend to relevant elements in visual material, incorporate graphic material into presentations, understand the importance of using graphic aids in different situations, and in general view the use of graphic aids in written or oral reporting as important assets to the overall presentation. These abilities, in turn, facilitate the students' effective interpretation and use of graphic aids in school.

Students must learn to use and interpret graphic aids accurately, and this is best accomplished through regular exposure to the various examples found in school and home materials such as books, magazines, and newspapers. Teachers can provide ongoing assistance with the development of this study skill by helping students to identify key elements within graphic aids and by relating the importance of the visual material to the overall context in which it appears. Study skills problems with graphic aids will be most evident as students attempt to interpret and apply meaning to visual material; however, problems may also relate to the development and use of graphic aids to complete different assigned tasks. Some indicators of problems associated with graphic aids are addressed in the Guide for Identifying Graphic Aids Needs (Form 5.3). The Visual Material Guide–Student Form (Form 5.4) is a student reference sheet for developing and studying visual material.

Graphic Aids: Best Practices

- Instruct students to bring maps of their community to school, and challenge them to find the shortest route to various places.
- After providing students with a visual aid, ask questions that can only be answered correctly by accurately studying and interpreting the visual aid.
- Instruct students to study only the pictures accompanying a reading passage. After a few minutes of study, they should write what they believe to be the main ideas in the material.
- Instruct students to find examples and explain different types of graphs (e.g., picture, circle, pie, bar, line).
- Provide students with different types of maps (e.g., road, political, weather), and have learners identify the similarities and differences found in each.
- Instruct students to make and label their own visual aids.
- Provide students with some written material and instruct them to develop graphic aids for the material.

- Require at least one graphic aid with selected written or oral reports.
- Periodically allow the use of graphic presentations as alternatives to oral and written reports.
- Discuss with students why material is presented graphically.
- Through leading questions, assist students to focus on key features of graphic material.
- Allow students sufficient time to read and interpret graphic aids as they are being presented.

Guide for Identifying Graphic Aids Needs

Student Name _____

Completed by _____ Date _____

Directions: Check the box next to each behavior that the student exhibits on a regular and consistent basis. Summarize the areas of need to complete the guide.

- ☐ Is unable to identify main elements within visual material

- ☐ Is unable to determine the connection between visual material and printed text

- ☐ Pays undue attention to less important elements of a visual aid

- ☐ Fails to understand the general purposes for including visual material in written and oral presentations

- ☐ Uses graphic material in presentations in ways that do not contribute to the topic presented

- ☐ Finds it difficult or is reluctant to develop and use graphic aids when completing various assignments

- ☐ Fails to study graphic aids or visuals that increase understanding of a topic being read (e.g., does not use picture clues to increase comprehension)

- ☐ Frequently misinterprets visual aids due to a lack of understanding of the items or units of measurement depicted

- ☐ Spends insufficient amount of time trying to interpret graphic aids, resulting in frequent skimming over of visual material

- ☐ Frequently loses concentration or has difficulty getting back on task after viewing and studying graphic aids

Summary comments: _____

_____

_____

_____

Visual Material Guide—Student Form

Name _____ Date _____

Title of visual _____

Place visual is found _____

Directions: Respond to the following questions in your own words as you develop or study the visual material.

What is the material depicting?

What are the most important aspects of the visual material?

What are the supporting elements in the visual material?

How does the visual material relate to what is being said or read?

How does the visual material enhance understanding of the topic being discussed or read?

To what extent does the caption or title of the material reflect what is depicted in the visual?

Does the visual material contain too much information?

Does the visual material contain too little information?

What questions come to mind while studying the visual material?

In what other ways might the same information be depicted?

What is the overall purpose of the visual material?

Library Usage: Easy Access to Information

The critical elements of this study skill are

- Understanding the overall functions, purposes, and value of a library
- Knowledge of the Internet in library usage
- Understanding and using the cataloging system
- Efficiently locating library materials
- Recognizing the types of assistance available to users

Importance of Library Usage in School

Students are periodically required to use library facilities to complete or participate in various activities. Throughout their formal schooling, students need to develop, maintain, and refine their library skills. Libraries provide one of the most intellectually stimulating places students may visit to acquire knowledge and access information.

Using the school or classroom library effectively provides unparalleled advantages in students' development. Libraries and their offerings ensure that students will be able to know more than just the events and issues specific to their own generations. In addition, libraries enable students to begin a search for information in a place that has a multitude of materials.

Libraries provide students with a variety of activities, such as story hours, poetry reading sessions, puppet shows, movies, and special interest activities. In support of these and similar activities, libraries contain numerous types of reading and reference materials, including the following:

- Encyclopedias and reference materials
- Films, filmstrips, and interactive videos
- Fiction and nonfiction books
- Self-help resources and material
- Newspapers, magazines, and journals
- Educational program kits
- Computer software
- CD-ROM equipment and archives
- Internet access and use

The importance of library usage in schools stems from the fact that each of these reading and reference materials contains information necessary to complete a variety of required tasks, particularly research papers. The library activities provide positive and interesting learning experiences for students, whether they are engaged in them to complete school requirements or simply for the sake of participating in recreational areas of interest. Although this vital avenue for learning exists, many students never fully appreciate the value of a library.

Elements of Library Usage

Appreciating a classroom, school, or community library begins with an understanding of various elements in a library. Effective use of a library includes knowledge of at least four elements:

- The services a library has to offer
- The types of information available in a library
- Procedures for locating sources in the library
- The types of assistance available to library users

An understanding of these elements indicates an understanding of why libraries exist and why a person might use one. Students need to understand why it is appropriate and beneficial to use libraries to complete school-related tasks or for personal and recreational purposes. Once this understanding has been internalized, students will be motivated and more likely to continue using library facilities.

To a great extent, successful use of a library contributes to an understanding of its benefits and applications. One of the greatest problem areas associated with library usage occurs when students are expected to use a library without preparation for what sources exist and how to locate them. Understanding the library's physical layout and the system for locating information should be developed in students prior to expecting extensive library usage. This preparation will minimize frustration and maximize efficiency.

The ability to locate information in a library requires knowledge of the cataloging system, including online access, and of the physical organization of resources. In reference to physical layout, most libraries post signs, maps, or other types of indicators to identify where materials reside. Students should review these visual aids prior to beginning an information search and refer to them while seeking sources. After several visits, most students acquire a general understanding of the library and can locate materials quickly.

A much more difficult task in library usage is learning and understanding the catalog system. Specifically, students need to learn the subject and author cataloguing systems (computer or card) and the Dewey Decimal and Library of Congress cataloging systems. Students must become proficient in locating materials by subject and author and familiar with each of the two major classification systems.

Students also need to become familiar with personnel who assist library users. The librarian or media specialist is often the person called upon in schools to educate students about why libraries exist, how to locate information through the card catalog or computer system, and how the facility is laid out. In times of need or difficulty in locating information, the librarian or media specialist is the person to consult. This person also helps students identify the types of materials available to address a particular topic. Students should feel comfortable consulting the media specialist regarding questions or problems about the library.

Identifying Library Usage Needs

Students who possess adequate library skills are not intimidated by cataloguing systems or large collections of books and resources, and they are willing users of library facilities for both required and leisure purposes. Their efficient practice of this study skill is seen in many areas of their school and personal lives. These students can complete library assignments effectively, whether drawing on one source or numerous references to satisfy the task.

Understanding and using a library are skills that students can tap throughout their lives. Through support and encouragement, teachers can assist students in skills development and continued reliance on classroom, school, and community libraries. Requiring students to use the library often at school facilitates more complete assignments and fosters continued interest in library resources for future assignments. Students who have difficulty with the library may exhibit a variety of problem indicators, but many of these relate to their unwilling or inefficient use of the facilities. The Guide for Identifying Library Usage Needs (Form 5.5) addresses some of these indicators.

Library Usage: Best Practices

- Emphasize the use and importance of the library and its resources in the overall educational program.
- Familiarize students with the functions and organization of the classroom, school, and local libraries.
- Periodically require the use of library resources in assigned tasks.
- Ensure that students are aware of the specific purpose of using the library when assigned a library activity.
- Encourage students to use media specialists and other library personnel as necessary.
- Instruct students to make visual displays that show how to use the electronic library catalog system and reference materials, and that enumerate the proper steps for locating and checking out library material (Wallace & Kauffman, 1990). Tell students to include the use of computerized systems and the Internet for locating library materials.
- Provide students with an index card containing one or more key terms about a specific concept. Instruct them to use online services to identify various sources that provide additional information about the concept.
- Develop a classroom library, complete with an electronic cataloging system.
- Provide students with a library assignment, instructing them to explain the location in the library of the materials they used to complete the assignment.
- Following a computer search, explain the computer printout and instruct each student to find an article or document listed on the printout.
- Instruct students to display graphically the organization of their school library, highlighting the location of different resources and materials.

Guide for Identifying Library Usage Needs

Student Name _____

Completed by _____ Date _____

Directions: Check the box next to each behavior that the student exhibits on a regular and consistent basis. Summarize the areas of need to complete the guide.

☐ Cannot locate sources in cataloging system

☐ Demonstrates continued confusion about physical layout of library facility

☐ Fails to seek help from librarian or media specialist, resulting in failure to find necessary source of information

☐ Lacks knowledge about various library services after frequent use of the library

☐ Habitually selects topics for research paper assignments that require little use of the library

☐ Uses library to complete assignments only when required

☐ Demonstrates a general lack of understanding of why a library should be used

☐ Is unable to locate sources after identifying them in the cataloging system

☐ Rarely visits a library for personal or leisure activities

☐ Is generally unwilling to use the library, which interferes with overall learning

Summary comments: _____

_____

_____

_____

Reference Materials: Using the Right Sources

The critical elements of this study skill are

- Knowing the purposes of different reference materials
- Using reference materials appropriately when necessary
- Using the Internet to gather information
- Using a variety of technologies (Internet, CD-ROM) to gather information
- Incorporating information into class assignments or everyday life needs
- Helping individuals cope with the demands of an information society

Importance of Reference Materials in School

After locating information and sources in the library, students need to know how to use the materials. Reference materials provide students with information about a seemingly unlimited number of topics. Knowledge about how best to use these sources helps to transform large and comprehensive books into manageable materials containing a variety of ideas, facts, or topics specific to particular assignments. However, reference materials only help students if they know how and for what purposes to use them; otherwise, the material serves no practical purpose.

Stated simply, reference materials help students to learn, solve problems, complete assignments, develop interests, and understand the world in which they live. A variety of classroom tasks may require reference materials, some directly related to specific subjects and others assigned to provide practice in the materials' use. Reference materials help to complete a variety of individual and group projects, such as the following:

- Supplemental reports detailing a specific topic of interest
- Semester research papers or projects
- Locating places around the home, city, state, country, or world
- Identifying specific facts about a topic
- Keeping current with a variety of issues or topics
- Developing a greater understanding of a hobby or other area of interest
- Learning about the lives of other people from around the world
- Documenting historical or chronological events

Students should be guided in their efforts to learn about issues and topics through the effective use of this study skill.

Elements Related to Reference Materials

Students must learn the following steps to use reference materials effectively:

1. Identify possible appropriate sources.
2. Determine the appropriateness of a source once it has been selected and located.

3. Review the information in the source efficiently.

4. Document necessary information from the source for future reference and inclusion in a project report or activity.

Once a potential topic has been identified for further study, students face the task of determining the most appropriate sources for gathering information about the topic. Identifying appropriate sources begins with identifying the type of information desired. In some instances this may include first locating very general information, either to help narrow down a topic or to determine if one desires to pursue a topic in greater detail. In other situations the purpose for using reference materials is to document more detailed information about a topic already selected and delineated. Whatever the reason for turning to reference materials, however, students should determine the purpose prior to engaging in the location process, to minimize time wasted locating inappropriate or unnecessary materials. Once students identify the type of information desired, they can better zero in on the most appropriate source(s) from which to gather their information. Examples of types of information (and appropriate sources for initial consultation) include the following:

- Definition of words (dictionary)

- Appropriate words or synonyms (thesaurus)

- Collections of titles about a specific topic (various index sources, microfiche)

- Location of a place (atlas, map)

- Biographical information (encyclopedia, CD-ROM)

- Current events (recent newspapers or magazines, online service)

- General or detailed information about a topic (encyclopedia, videos, CD-ROM, filmstrips, the Internet, online service)

These and other purposes for using reference materials guide decisions pertaining to their appropriate selection. Although a variety of sources may be used to address different topics, the most direct ones should be consulted initially to ensure the best results.

Once sources have been identified and located, students must determine quickly whether they are the right ones for the intended use (i.e., whether the sources contain the desired information). To complete this task, students need to apply skills such as skimming and scanning; using guide words, the table of contents, or the index; reviewing headings and subheadings; and alphabetizing. Rather than reading entire books at this point, students must quickly and efficiently review the selected sources to determine their appropriateness for the task. Much research time can be wasted reviewing potential sources that are expected to contain the necessary information when, in fact, they do not.

When the student has determined through a general and quick overview that a source is useful for a particular topic, the tasks of reviewing and documenting the necessary information begin. When completing these tasks, students should keep in mind several points and document information accordingly:

- Record the information from one source on the same piece of paper or index card, fastening together pages or cards if several are needed for one source.

- Develop and follow a consistent format for documenting information from each reference source (e.g., author, date, title, publisher information).

- Record the catalog number for quick relocation of the source.

- Record only essential information needed for the topic or assignment (other information may be of interest but should be recorded at this time only if appropriate to the particular task).

- Record information accurately the first time to minimize wasting time going back to a source.

- Be certain that quotes are documented accurately, including page number(s).

- File cards or papers in an organized, logical, and protected manner to minimize loss of material and ensure easy future reference.

- Prior to leaving the source and filing the documented information, reread what was documented from the source to make certain that it can be easily interpreted and understood at a later time.

As students work through these steps, other related study skills come into play (e.g., library usage, notetaking and outlining, varying reading rates, graphic aids) and will contribute to the overall effective implementation of this study skill. Effective implementation of this skill in turn facilitates the proper use of others, such as report writing and oral presentations.

Identifying Reference Materials Needs

Students who use reference materials effectively select the right sources, waste little time reviewing their sources, document the essential information in a consistent and meaningful format, document all needed information from sources the first time the task is undertaken, and file their recorded information in an efficient manner. Students are required to use reference materials for a variety of assignments in school. After making assignments, teachers need to ensure that students know how to use reference materials to complete the tasks. Students must be taught where to find reference materials, why they are used, and how to use them in ways that minimize wasted time and energy. Some indicators of problems associated with reference materials usage are addressed in the Guide for Identifying Reference Materials Needs (Form 5.6).

The Reference Materials Form (Form 5.7) assists students in recording essential information found in reference materials for use in report writing or oral presentations. The general information about the reference material should be recorded, including the Internet information, for easy access to that material if necessary. In addition, one or more key words reflecting the information should be recorded (e.g., *kite, rivers, wheat farming*). This information is followed by a concise summary of the essential information relative to the topic in question. This should be specific enough to explain the main points to be included in the report. The summary is followed by a brief statement reflecting the specific use of the information in the report (i.e., how this information relates to the topic). The completed forms may be cataloged by the key words and arranged in the proper order when report development begins. Other related sources also may be listed in the reference materials, and enough information should be documented so the student can easily locate the sources later. Finally, space is provided for any additional comments that come to mind as the student is documenting reference material information. This type of form allows students to document important information found in reference materials accurately and methodically.

Once completed, the forms may be filed easily in a notebook for future reference. When students have gathered sufficient information about the topic, they can develop the actual report. The key words on the forms, along with the statement reflecting the specific use of the information in the report, serve as guides to organize the report. The summaries and comments then are compiled and expanded upon as the full report takes shape.

Reference Materials Usage: Best Practices

- Instruct students to provide their own definition of a word and compare it with the definition in an online dictionary (Harris & Sipay, 1990).
- Teach students how to use online search engines (e.g., Google) for finding information, images, news, and other resources.
- Assign students tasks that require the use of the Internet to gather information.
- Assign students tasks that facilitate the use of Microsoft Word along with dictionary.com.
- Provide students with the name of a place and ask them to identify the different types of information that various reference sites supply about the place (e.g., atlas, encyclopedia).
- Instruct students to look up selected words in a dictionary and identify the guide words on each page.
- Provide students with some information about a specific topic within a larger reading selection. Instruct them to identify from the index the entry word(s) most appropriate to gain more information about the topic.
- Supply students with various questions and ask them to identify the reference materials they might consult to answer the questions.
- Assign a small group of students one topic that requires use of various online resources. Give each student in the group a task for which different online resources are needed. After they complete the tasks, have the students share the type of information gathered from their respective sources.
- Ensure that all students have a dictionary readily available for their use.
- Provide assignments that require use of the Internet to find necessary information.
- Provide opportunities to use numerous print resources (e.g., atlas, yellow pages).

Guide for Identifying Reference Materials Needs

Student Name _____

Completed by _____ Date _____

Directions: Check the box next to each behavior that the student exhibits on a regular and consistent basis. Summarize the areas of need to complete the guide.

- ☐ Takes unusually long periods of time to locate information reference material

- ☐ Continually consults inappropriate reference materials when completing assignments

- ☐ Continually needs to return to the same reference source to gather necessary information rather than documenting most or all of the needed information the first time the source is reviewed

- ☐ Spends excessive amount of time determining the suitability of material for the project in question

- ☐ Infrequently consults major reference sources such as dictionaries, maps, encyclopedias, CD-ROMs, the Internet, or online services

- ☐ Cannot explain the procedures to follow to use reference materials effectively

- ☐ Follows an inconsistent format for recording reference material information

- ☐ Frequently records inaccurate or incomplete information from reference material

- ☐ Frequently records information that is irrelevant to the topic or task in question

- ☐ Develops note cards that are not useful for future study or reference

Summary comments: _____

_____

_____

_____

Reference Materials Form

Name _____ Date _____

Subject area _____

Reference material _____

Catalog number _____

Internet address _____

Name of article _____

Author _____

Publisher _____

Volume/year _____ Pages _____

KEY WORDS _____

Summary: _____

_____

_____

Specific use in report: _____

_____

_____

Related sources: _____

_____

_____

Additional comments: _____

_____

_____

Performance Standards

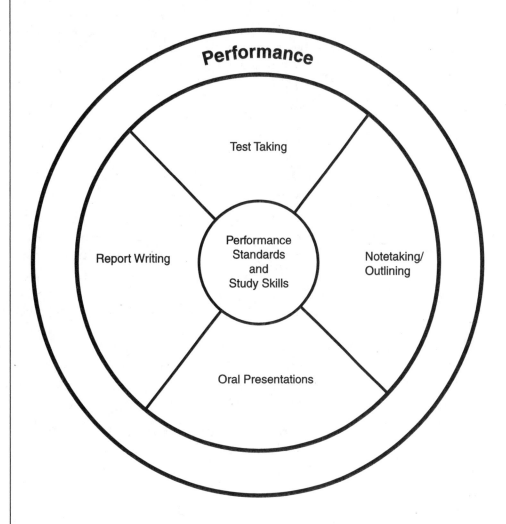

Test Taking: Improving Test Performance

The critical elements of this study skill are

- Reading and understanding directions
- Identifying and correcting test-taking errors
- Organizing written responses
- Identifying and using clue words
- Correcting previous test-taking errors
- Recording responses properly

Importance of Test Taking in School

Students are subjected to various forms of testing almost from the day they enter school. In addition, in recent years the pressures placed on students to perform well on tests have increased. Results from tests are used to determine grade promotion, graduation, and entrance into college, as well as mid-semester and end-of-year grades. Tests usually mark the end of a course or unit of study. After studying and acquiring knowledge, students have to provide some indication of competence related to that knowledge. In recent years, the acceptable minimum level of competence has increased in many states and school districts throughout the country. As a result, students must be better prepared in content and skills as well as in test-taking abilities. Specifically, test taking and test-taking skills are important in school for the following reasons:

- Test results provide an indication of students' particular skills and abilities.
- Students' test results are frequently compared with other scores from around the country.
- Weekly quizzes help to identify areas in which students require additional work prior to the end-of-unit test.
- Test results provide one basis for determining grades.
- Course grades, which are based to a great extent on test results, become very important if students pursue postsecondary education.
- Test results may be used to determine levels of expectation for individual students.

The emphasis placed on test taking in school reflects the importance of ensuring that students perform as well as possible on tests. In addition to employing the other study skills discussed in this book to learn and retain information, a variety of test-taking skills will help students perform as well as possible on essay or objective tests.

Elements Related to Test Taking

In addition to the use of other study skills to learn information, students need to learn three major components of test taking: preparing and studying for the test, taking the test, and reviewing results and test-taking strategies once the test has been graded.

Preparing and Studying for the Test

In preparing and studying for a test, students should complete several sequential tasks:

1. List all the topics that will be on the test.
2. Organize notes related to each topic.
3. Gather primary and supplemental reading materials that will be used to study each topic.
4. Prioritize topics in order of importance to ensure that the main topics receive sufficient emphasis.
5. Assess the current level of preparation for each topic to help determine how much time will be needed for studying or reviewing each topic.
6. Designate specific amounts of time required to study each topic, based on current levels of preparation.
7. Establish a timetable for studying each topic.
8. Begin studying procedures following the timelines established, ensuring that the major topics are studied initially.

These tasks apply to studying for any type of test, whether a weekly quiz or a major semester test.

Important in the process of studying for a test is the ability to anticipate questions about different topics. Although test takers cannot necessarily predict exact questions, test takers can identify general types of questions fairly accurately. Using knowledge about the content, instructor, and amount of emphasis or coverage of different subtopics, test takers should produce and answer anticipated test questions while studying related information. Although students should not rely excessively on anticipated questions while studying, these do assist in overall preparation for a test.

In summary, the process of preparing and studying for a test includes organizing notes and reading material, determining topics to study, identifying projected amounts of time required to prepare for the test, and generating and answering various questions to address the topics on the test. Depending on the frequency with which tests are taken (e.g., weekly, monthly, quarterly), preparations should begin well in advance of the examination date. The amount of time required will vary from student to student, but plans and procedures for studying should begin relatively soon after the coverage of the topic begins and the test date is known.

Taking the Test

The following test-taking strategies help ensure the most accurate test results:

- Read all directions carefully, ensuring that they are understood.

- Skim the entire test prior to responding to the items.

- Save the more difficult questions until the easier items have been answered.

- Place a check in the margin next to any items skipped or those to review if time permits.

- Estimate each calculation prior to performing the actual calculation. This assists in eliminating obviously wrong answers and provides a general figure that should approximate the final, more detailed calculation.

- Identify and use clue words in items. These are words that help to narrow down the correct response (e.g., *never, always, usually*) or reveal the type of essay response required (e.g., *list, evaluate, critique*).

- Properly record each answer on objective tests (i.e., multiple choice, true/false, matching).

- Use proper grammar and sentence structure in essay responses, ensuring that answers are well organized and complete.

- Construct the first sentence of an essay question response to directly answer the question, using some of the same words found in the actual question.

- Narrow correct responses whenever possible to eliminate obviously wrong answers.

- Look for clues in other questions to help respond to those items of which you are uncertain.

- Prior to submitting the completed test, review and proofread the responses for neatness, completed answers, and proper recording on answer sheets.

- Avoid changing answers arbitrarily. Responses should be changed only for very good and sound reasons, based on information that may be realized after the item was answered initially.

In addition to these test-taking and preparation strategies, students should be familiar with the following types of items and know which are used on the test.

- *Essay* items require a narrative response that may range from a couple of paragraphs to several pages.

- *Short-answer* items are similar in style to essay items except they are restricted in length of response.

- *Sentence completion* items provide a partial statement that must be completed to make a correct response.

- *Matching* items contain a variety of responses, each of which must be correctly matched (these often are presented in a two-column format).

- *Multiple-choice* items contain a statement, followed by several choices from which the respondent must select the best possible answer.

- *True/false* items contain a complete statement for which the respondent must indicate true or false (if any part of the statement is false, the entire statement is false, even though some parts may be true).

Responses to essay, short-answer, and sentence completion items must be based on content recalled by students with little or no assistance from the questions. Generating a brief outline or writing down key words that come to mind after reading these types of items assists with recalling information necessary to respond successfully to the items. Students should bear this in mind when studying for these types of items.

Matching, multiple-choice, and true/false items provide more information in the questions than do essay or short-answer items. In any of these, particularly matching questions, much of the information necessary to respond to the item is provided; test takers need only sort it out. In addition, the content found in questions and response choices may provide clues for correct responses to other test items. Therefore, these types of objective test questions may provide or trigger awareness of responses to other items. Students should not overly rely on these test-taking strategies, for they in no way substitute for proper test preparation and learning of material. They may, however, assist in identifying correct responses to some items on a test, once material has been learned and retained.

Reviewing Results and Test-Taking Strategies

After receiving graded tests back from teachers, students should review their test results and the strategies they used to study for and take the test. Students should review correct and incorrect responses in an attempt to identify why the items were right or wrong. Review of studying procedures, notetaking strategies, and test-taking skills helps students to determine if problems lie in the initial acquisition of the information (e.g., through lectures and readings), in the procedures for studying for the test, or in errors made while taking the test. Students should look for patterns that indicate test-taking strengths or weaknesses and then continue with those strategies that appear to be effective and change those that are ineffective. Although students may not determine reasons for correct or incorrect responses for every item, they may be able to identify general test-taking skills if they are used regularly.

Identifying Test-Taking Needs

Students with effective test-taking skills know how to study for different types of tests, understand the various types of test items, systematically and regularly apply appropriate test-taking skills when completing a test, review tests once they have been completed, and learn from their previous test-taking errors by not making similar mistakes on future tests. As previously emphasized, effective test-taking skills do not compensate for not knowing the material covered on a test. They may, however, help students minimize careless and costly errors related to preparing for, completing, and reviewing tests.

When a student lacks proficiency in test-taking skills, the effects of proficiency in other study skills areas may be lessened. Although not a substitute for knowing the material, effective test-taking skills ensure that students will have the best possible chance to show what they know. One of the greatest tragedies of effective and efficient studying is the inability of some students to demonstrate the knowledge they possess because of poor test-taking skills.

Ongoing efforts between teachers and students to develop and maintain test-taking skills will prove beneficial to all concerned in both short- and long-term educational situations. As test-taking skills intermingle with other study skills, students develop the best chance to succeed no matter what type of testing situation they encounter. Given the various types of tests used in schools, along with the different strategies available for studying for and reviewing tests, a variety of indicators may suggest problems with test taking. Several of these are addressed in the Guide for Identifying Test-Taking Needs (Form 5.8), which is followed by four test-taking references for student use in the classroom.

The Test Preparation Guide–Student Form (Form 5.9) lists a variety of items to consider when preparing for any test. These items help students to study for tests in a more systematic manner, which improves overall test performance. The Studying for Tests Form (Form 5.10) provides a simple-to-use format for recording information necessary to study for a specific test. The Objective Tests Review Guide–Student Form (Form 5.11) and the Essay Tests Review Guide–Student Form (Form 5.12) identify points to consider when reviewing completed tests. Through systematic review of test results, students may identify and correct test-taking errors and thereby improve future test performance.

In addition to completing the Test Preparation Guide–Student Form (Form 5.9) while preparing for tests, students should complete the Studying for Tests Form (Form 5.10) to ensure that they adequately study the major topics to be covered on the test. To complete this guide, students list the major topics to be included on the test. These are categorized into primary and secondary topics. The primary topics include those areas central to the content or skill areas being assessed and often include the issues most heavily emphasized by the instructor or reading material. They are the topics essential to understanding the issues, skills, or concepts on the test. The secondary topics include the supporting issues or concepts that provide additional understanding once the primary issues have been learned. They are important to acquiring a more complete understanding of the issues, skills, or concepts but are not necessarily essential to learning a topic. The primary topics should receive the most emphasis when studying for a test.

After identifying and categorizing the topics, students should record how adequately prepared they believe they are at the time they complete the study guide (i.e., *very adequate, adequate, not adequate*). This self-assessment provides students a way to begin to prioritize the time necessary to study each topic. The primary topics receiving a *not adequate* rating should receive the highest priority for studying, followed by the other primary topics and the least prepared-for secondary topics. The topics receiving a *very adequate* or *adequate* rating should be reviewed regularly to maintain the knowledge. While completing the ratings, the students should also record the tasks they need to do to best prepare for each topic. Tasks may range from performing a general overview to thoroughly reviewing notes or reading material, depending on how adequately prepared students believe they are as they begin studying. Finally, students need to determine the approximate amount of time needed to study each topic. This may range from several days to a few minutes, depending on prior preparation levels. Continued use of Form 5.10 helps students to organize their time and prioritize activities in a systematic and structured way as they prepare for various types of tests.

Test Taking: Best Practices

- Show students how to take different types of tests.
- Explain different methods of study and types of materials necessary to study for objective and essay tests.
- Explore with students the purposes for taking tests.
- Review completed tests with students, highlighting test-taking errors.
- Ensure that students know how much time is allotted for completion of each test.
- Explore test-taking procedures with students, explaining different types of questions.
- Provide students with sample questions from various types of tests (e.g., multiple choice, true/false, essay) and discuss how students might approach each type of question to obtain an answer.
- Identify and discuss vocabulary terms often found in test directions (e.g., *compare, contrast, match, evaluate*) (Mercer & Mercer, 2000).
- Instruct students to write on the test form any facts or formulas they memorized previously, as well as ideas that may pertain to specific questions.
- Present and discuss the following test-taking guidelines for completing multiple-choice items: Know the number and kind of answers to select, remember the question, narrow the possibilities by eliminating obviously wrong answers, and record each answer carefully.
- Provide students with sample test questions, instructing them to indicate how they obtained the answers and to identify possible clues in the questions.
- Instruct students to outline reading material to be covered in an exam and anticipate potential essay, true/false, or multiple-choice questions.
- Review previous tests with students and discuss possible ways their performances may be improved through test-taking hints.
- Instruct students to generate different types of test questions from the same material. Discuss similarities and differences in the type of information required to answer each question.
- Familiarize students with general test-taking guidelines, which include reviewing the entire test, knowing allotted time to complete the test, knowing the value of different test items, reading and rereading the directions and questions, identifying clue words in questions, and responding to more difficult items after answering the easier questions.

Teaching Study Skills to Students with Learning Problems

Guide for Identifying Test-Taking Needs

Student Name _____

Completed by _____ Date _____

Directions: Check the box next to each behavior that the student exhibits on a regular and consistent basis. Summarize the areas of need to complete the guide.

☐ Is unable to effectively prioritize topics for studying

☐ Is unable to effectively plan and maintain a timeline for studying for a test

☐ Demonstrates poor organization of essay question responses

☐ Spends too much time initially attempting to answer more difficult questions on a test

☐ Inconsistently applies appropriate test-taking tips when completing a test

☐ Is unable to correct previous test-taking errors

☐ Guesses at answers prior to systematically narrowing the choices in a question

☐ Changes a large number of correct answers to incorrect responses

☐ Has difficulty budgeting time to complete a test, resulting in questions being unattempted or un-answered

☐ Ignores or does not use clue words within items

☐ Fails to proofread narrative responses

☐ Does not read or understand directions prior to beginning a test

Summary comments: _____

_____

_____

_____

Test Preparation Guide—Student Form

Name _____ Date _____

Test subject area _____ Test date _____

Directions: Check the box next to each item once you complete it in your preparation for the test. Information pertaining to some of the items is frequently provided by instructors, and you should ask your teachers if necessary.

- ☐ Organize notes

- ☐ Document or list all primary and secondary topics to be covered on the test

- ☐ From the list of topics to be covered, identify those you know the most and least about

- ☐ For each topic, determine what you need to do to best prepare for that part of the test (e.g., review notes, memorize terms or formulas, complete sample items)

- ☐ Determine the approximate amount of time needed to study each topic to be covered on the test

- ☐ Know the type of test and test items (e.g., multiple choice, matching, essay, short answer, true/false)

- ☐ Anticipate potential test questions that the instructor or test makers may ask

- ☐ Know what type of scoring will be used (e.g., partial credit for some items, points deducted for wrong answers, full or no credit only)

- ☐ Begin to prepare for the test well in advance of the test date

- ☐ Know the relative importance of the test as it pertains to the final grade in the course or class and study accordingly (e.g., 50% of final grade, weekly quiz accounting for only 5% of grade)

- ☐ Review each completed test to identify test-taking errors and correct these prior to the next test situation

- ☐ Know which topics account for the majority of the test and which are least important, and ensure that the appropriate amount of study time is spent on the most important topics

Studying for Tests Form

Name _____ Date _____

Subject area of test _____

Directions: Complete each column for each primary and secondary topic in the subject area.

Primary Topics	Preparation (*Very Adequate, Adequate, Not Adequate*)	Tasks to Complete to Study Topic	Estimated Time to Complete Tasks

(continues)

FORM 5.10 *Continued.*

Studying for Tests Form

Secondary Topics	Preparation (*Very Adequate, Adequate, Not Adequate*)	Tasks to Complete to Study Topic	Estimated Time to Complete Tasks

Additional comments about topics or test: _____

_____

_____

Objective Tests Review Guide—Student Form

Name _____ Date _____

Test reviewed _____

Directions: Check Yes or No for each item as you review the multiple-choice, matching, and true/false test items. Summarize your responses to complete the guide.

Did you . . .

Yes No

☐ ☐ Read each question carefully?

☐ ☐ Review all test questions prior to beginning answers?

☐ ☐ Respond to the more difficult or unknown items last?

☐ ☐ Identify and use clue words in items?

☐ ☐ Logically eliminate wrong answers in items?

☐ ☐ Estimate all calculations prior to beginning more thorough calculations?

☐ ☐ Make certain that all answers were recorded accurately?

☐ ☐ Place a check mark next to items initially left unanswered for quick return to those items?

☐ ☐ Change answers ONLY for very good and specific reasons?

☐ ☐ Narrow possible correct responses prior to final selection?

☐ ☐ Correct prior test-taking errors?

☐ ☐ Reread and check all answers prior to submitting test to instructor?

☐ ☐ Seek out necessary information to understand incorrect items?

☐ ☐ Identify your test-taking errors, if any?

☐ ☐ Identify your test-studying errors, if any?

Summary of review of test: Number of Yes responses _____

Number of No responses _____

Essay Tests Review Guide—Student Form

Name _____ Date _____

Test reviewed _____

Directions: Check Yes or No for each item as you review the narrative short-answer or essay test items. Summarize your responses to complete the guide.

Yes No

☐ ☐ The facts in each response are accurate and well organized.

☐ ☐ The content in each response is directly relevant to the question.

☐ ☐ My responses are sufficiently complete to fully answer the question.

☐ ☐ I used proper grammar, sentence structure, and punctuation.

☐ ☐ Each response is outlined briefly prior to its completion.

☐ ☐ All elements in the brief outlines are included in the responses.

☐ ☐ I responded to the easiest essay items initially.

☐ ☐ I carefully read all questions prior to beginning any responses.

☐ ☐ My responses include the instructor's main points regarding the topic.

☐ ☐ My responses are clearly written, avoiding vague generalizations.

☐ ☐ My first sentence in each response directly answers the question, followed by supporting details.

☐ ☐ I summarized the response for each question in one or two concluding sentences.

☐ ☐ I identified questions worth the most points and spent the appropriate amount of time completing them.

☐ ☐ I identified and corrected prior test-taking errors.

☐ ☐ I proofread responses prior to submitting the test to the instructor.

☐ ☐ I sought out information necessary to understand incorrect items.

Summary of review of test: Number of Yes responses _____

Number of No responses _____

Notetaking and Outlining: Capturing the Main Points

The critical elements of this study skill are

- Using headings appropriately
- Recording essential information
- Organizing notes well
- Taking clear and concise notes

Importance of Notetaking and Outlining in School

Study skills associated with listening and reading can improve significantly as students develop and master notetaking and outlining abilities. Notetaking and outlining require students to document major ideas and important points for reference in future study of a topic. The process includes summarizing and organizing information into a format that captures main ideas related to what is heard or read.

Effective notetaking and outlining skills must be employed by elementary and secondary students to study and subsequently learn the various skills, topics of information, and general knowledge necessary for grade promotion and successful achievement testing. Notetaking and outlining assist in a variety of educational tasks:

- Recording lecture information
- Reading and completing school assignments
- Reading texts and supplemental books
- Studying for tests
- Organizing complex material
- Completing written or oral reports

Elements Related to Notetaking and Outlining

Effective notetaking and outlining require that students can do the following:

- Write brief and clear notes
- Use headings and subheadings appropriately
- Use abbreviations that are meaningful for future reference
- Determine the difference between main and supporting ideas in order to record the most essential information for the particular notetaking or outlining task
- Summarize information in a meaningful manner
- Document information in short phrases rather than full sentences
- Attend as closely to the end of the notetaking or outlining activity as to the beginning of the session
- Identify and record clue words or phrases in a lecture or reading activity in which notes are taken or outlines generated
- Develop a systematic method for notetaking or outlining and use the method on a consistent basis

Notetaking and outlining abilities require continued development and will improve through practice. Effective notetaking and outlining skills increase concentration and attention to lecture situations and provide structure to reading activities. Students who take notes and complete outlines of little or no use for future study or reference require specific and guided practice to (a) learn how to take notes, (b) construct meaningful outlines, (c) attend to relevant verbal or visual cues, and (d) understand the general purposes of taking notes and generating outlines. Teachers may identify indicators of potential problems through review of students' work and through discussions with students about how they take notes and why they believe they are important.

Although no specific format or procedure for taking notes is considered superior to others, some organized form of notetaking should occur during lecture situations. Also, many reading activities require that students write brief outlines or notes to fully grasp and retain meaning. More complex and detailed readings or lecture situations often require more complete notetaking or comprehensive outlines for future reference. Teachers provide vital support to school-related notetaking and outlining activities through ongoing assistance and review with students.

Identifying Notetaking and Outlining Needs

Problems associated with ineffective and deficient notetaking or outlining abilities are most apparent when students must refer to notes or outlines at a future time and find they are unable to use what they wrote in any meaningful way. Some indicators of potential notetaking and outlining problems are addressed on the Guide for Identifying Notetaking and Outlining Needs (Form 5.13). This guide is followed by two others designed for students to assist them with notetaking and outlining. The Notetaking Guide—Lectures (Form 5.14) provides a structure that is easy to follow in lecture situations. Students should use it to document key points in brief form and then to summarize them in narrative form following the lecture. The Chapter-Outlining Guide (Form 5.15) helps students to organize content found in their reading material. The guide includes four parts: main heading, subheadings, subheading summaries, and summary of main heading. Students document each main heading and associated subheadings, then briefly summarize each subheading. After summarizing the subheadings, the students compile them to reflect an overall summary of the associated main heading in the chapter. If more details from a particular heading or subheading are required once this form has been completed, the student reviews specific sections or pages within the chapter. A separate form should be used for each main heading that requires outlining.

Notetaking and Outlining: Best Practices

- Ensure that students follow a consistent format when outlining or taking notes.

- Assist students in identifying key topics and ideas.

- Discuss the uses and advantages of notetaking and outlining.

- Model various notetaking and outlining formats when presenting information to students.

- Begin with simple notetaking and outlining activities and gradually increase to more complex activities.

- Place an outline of a reading selection on the board, read the material with the students, and review and discuss the outline (Harris & Sipay, 1990).
- Instruct students to generate an outline of a major topic or story covered on a radio or television news program.
- Present a brief lecture and have the students take notes and compare these notes with each other.
- Place the complete skeleton of an outline for a reading selection on the board and fill in only the main headings. Instruct the students to read the selection and complete the outline (Harris & Sipay, 1990).
- Provide the students with a skeleton outline and a list of words pertaining to a topic. Instruct them to complete the outline to fit the list of words, generating main ideas, subheadings, and specific details.
- Present students with note cards that contain sufficient information to cover a brief topic. Instruct them to write a paragraph summarizing the contents of the note cards.
- Present students with a series of note cards that describe events pertaining to a topic. Scramble the cards and instruct the students to arrange them in proper sequence.
- Provide students with note cards that contain all information except topic headings. Have them read the cards and generate possible topic headings.
- Instruct students to read a passage and complete note cards for the selection.
- Assign peers to review their notes with other students after a lecture or other notetaking activity, to ensure that the essential information was documented.
- Pause periodically during a notetaking activity and tell the students what to record in their notes.

FORM 5.13

Guide for Identifying Notetaking and Outlining Needs

Student Name _____

Completed by _____ Date _____

Directions: Check the box next to each behavior that the student exhibits on a regular and consistent basis. Summarize the areas of need to complete the guide.

☐ Is unable to record or identify major points from a lecture or reading selection

☐ Consistently writes everything possible when notetaking rather than documenting only key points

☐ Is unable to study effectively from recorded lecture notes

☐ Uses inconsistent formats when taking notes

☐ Uses inconsistent formats when making outlines

☐ Omits key ideas when taking notes

☐ Is unable to capture an author's or lecturer's main ideas through notetaking

☐ Is unable to capture main ideas when outlining

☐ Continuously makes unorganized notes

☐ Attends too much to a speaker's mannerisms while taking notes

☐ Produces notes or outlines that reflect only facts and not the meaning underlying them

☐ Is unable to develop a meaningful style and format for taking clear and concise notes for use in future studying

Summary comments: _____

_____

_____

_____

Notetaking Guide—Lectures

Name _____ Teacher _____

Directions: In the spaces below, write the main ideas and supporting details from the lecture. Upon completion, summarize the overall lecture.

Subject _____

Date _____ Time _____

Specific topic covered in lecture _____

Main Ideas	Supporting Details					

Summary of lecture: _____

_____

_____

Chapter-Outlining Guide

Name _____ Date _____

Directions: In the spaces below, write key information about the book, main heading, and subheadings.

Book _____ Chapter _____

Topic _____ Pages _____

A. Main heading _____

B. Subheadings

C. Subheading Summaries

D. Summary of main heading (summarize all the subheadings from above): _____
_____
_____

Report Writing: Creating Better Written Reports

The critical elements of this study skill are

- Organizing thoughts in writing
- Using proper punctuation
- Using correct grammar
- Stating clear introductory and concluding statements

Importance of Report Writing in School

Producing a written report, whether a simple paragraph or an extended research paper, involves the ability to organize one's ideas and present them on paper in some organized and meaningful way. This process taps skills associated with grammar, punctuation, sentence structure, creative thinking, and handwriting, as well as skills related to library usage, reading rate, and using reference materials. Schoolwork often requires students to write various types of reports, and being able to write effectively helps students to complete their report writing tasks more efficiently.

One overall purpose of writing programs in school is to develop functional communication skills in writing. Written work highlights students' communication abilities and effective expression of ideas. Report writing is an essential study skill because students are frequently asked to communicate or express their ideas in writing. Assignments in this area of education may include tasks such as these:

- Writing a factual paper about a specific topic
- Providing a written critique about a story or event
- Evaluating, in writing, steps or procedures pertaining to a topic
- Writing an extensive research paper
- Summarizing the contents of a lecture or reading assignment

In addition to these and similar "formal" written report assignments, many other tasks in school require responding to issues, topics, stories, or activities in writing. Regardless of whether the written report is a short one- or two-paragraph response or a 15-page term paper, report-writing abilities must be applied. Also, computer use should be encouraged when appropriate to facilitate effective written reports.

Elements Related to Report Writing

When written reports are assigned, they usually include some instructions related to choice of topic, approximate length, and type of effort required (e.g., factual, opinion, critique, summary). The latitude provided to students surrounding instructions varies widely from teacher to teacher. As a result, the first major element to effective report writing is knowing the instructor's expectations and the type of report assigned. Then students can begin the process of actually writing the assigned report or paper, which includes these steps:

1. Selecting a topic
2. Identifying a particular subject area within that topic

3. Narrowing the topic
4. Investigating the topic
5. Writing the initial draft of the report
6. Editing and proofreading to complete the final version of the written report

When students select a topic, it is important that they choose an area of interest. Depending on the length and extent of the paper, much time and energy could be spent researching and writing it; therefore, greater interest in the topic makes the task more enjoyable and potentially easier. Similarly, the specific subject to be investigated within the general topic area should be of interest. Once the general topic has been selected and narrowed down to a particular subject area, investigation of that specific area begins. The actual investigation of the topic may involve a variety of activities:

- Library research
- Observation of something or someone related to the topic
- Interviewing someone associated with the topic
- Actual experience related to the topic
- Discussions with an expert via the Internet

The topics of using a library and using reference materials are discussed in detail previously in this chapter as separate study skills. If the students are engaged in observing or interviewing, of greatest concern is that they know exactly what it is they want to ask or look for during these types of activities. Using effective notetaking skills, such as those discussed previously, will facilitate use of the information gathered through interviewing or observing. If documentation related to actual experiences surrounding the topic is included in the report, students should be aware of the specific reasons for having the experiences and keep accurate records of the events or issues they encountered. When these events are well documented, they may be easily incorporated into the initial and final revisions of the written report, along with summaries of observations, interviews, and library research.

Identifying Report-Writing Needs

Students with effective report-writing skills are capable of selecting and narrowing a topic, possess sufficient mechanical writing abilities to complete initial and refined versions of a written report, and understand the purpose for each writing assignment. They also know the specific directions and instructions pertaining to each writing assignment prior to beginning the writing process.

The problem indicators addressed in the Guide for Identifying Report-Writing Needs (Form 5.16) reflect specific tasks related to writing reports. Poor report-writing skills also may result from deficient study skills related to library usage, reference material usage, notetaking and outlining, or even time management. Therefore, if students exhibit problems in writing or completing written reports, teachers may need to investigate problems with some of these other study skills areas along with the issues discussed in this section. Effective report-writing skills are essential to success in school at any grade level. Many students are quite capable of producing well-constructed written reports provided they receive necessary guidance concerning topic selection, use of proper writing mechanics, and other related study skills areas. By keeping in mind the specific elements associated with writing reports along with basic writing skills required to complete a written report, students can master this study skill. The Written Assignment Guide–Student Form (Form 5.17) lists items that students should consider when developing and reviewing written assignments prior to submission to the teacher.

Report Writing: Best Practices

- Clarify the specific purpose for the written assignment.
- Assist students in organizing their ideas.
- Begin with simple, less complex written assignments.
- Ensure that students proofread their written work.
- Encourage the use of a dictionary and other reference materials when necessary.
- Work with students as they progress through different stages of writing assignments (e.g., sentence and paragraph structure, outlining, formulating ideas).
- Provide periodic review and encouragement as written reports are completed.
- Review rules of punctuation and capitalization prior to beginning a written assignment.
- Instruct students to prepare written reports for the same topic and discuss advantages of different reporting styles.
- Provide students with a paragraph, omitting capital letters. Instruct the students to edit the paragraph and capitalize appropriate words.
- Instruct students to develop a monthly newspaper, ensuring that each student makes some contribution.
- Provide students with assignments that require summarizing longer material (Wallace & Kauffman, 1990).
- Instruct students to generate and share with each other letters similar to those found in newspaper editorial columns.
- Instruct students to record notes for a research paper on index cards and then sort them in proper sequence.
- Provide students with a paragraph containing both complete and incomplete sentences. Instruct them to identify each type.

FORM 5.16

Guide for Identifying Report-Writing Needs

Student Name _____

Completed by _____ Date _____

Directions: Check the box next to each behavior that the student exhibits on a regular and consistent basis. Summarize the areas of need to complete the guide.

☐ Is unable to select a topic for the report

☐ Selects topics in which he or she has little or no interest, resulting in either not completing or having great difficulty completing written reports

☐ Has difficulty organizing ideas in narrative form once notes and outlines have been completed

☐ Has difficulty narrowing a topic to a manageable size given the specific type of written assignment

☐ Has difficulty completing the initial draft of a report

☐ Is unable to refine the initial draft so proper grammar and sentence structure are used

☐ Takes unusually long periods of time to complete even the simplest written reports

☐ Cannot generate a clear introductory statement

☐ Cannot generate clear concluding statements in the report

☐ Often includes information not relevant to the topic

Summary comments: _____

_____

_____

_____

Written Assignment Guide—Student Form

Name _____ Date _____

Title of written assignment _____

Directions: Check each item if it accurately reflects your written assignment. This guide should be completed prior to submitting a final draft of the written assignment and after instructor feedback is obtained.

☐ Is the paper well organized?

☐ Is proper punctuation used?

☐ Is proper spelling used?

☐ Is proper grammar used?

☐ Is proper sentence structure used?

☐ Is the topic covered in sufficient detail?

☐ Does the paper contain all required elements, such as examples or charts and introductory and concluding sentences?

☐ Does the paper have a neat appearance?

☐ Was sufficient research completed to develop the paper in detail?

☐ Are footnotes and references used appropriately?

☐ Are quotations copied correctly?

☐ Does the paper have a clear beginning sentence?

☐ Does the paper have a clear concluding sentence?

☐ Are transitions from one idea to the next smooth and clear?

☐ Does the title reflect what the paper is about?

☐ Does the paper meet all requirements stipulated by the instructor?

Oral Presentations: Building Confidence

The critical elements of this study skill are

- Regularly participating in oral reporting activities
- Speaking clearly and in an organized way
- Using gestures appropriately

Importance of Oral Presentations in School

One of the most potentially difficult situations students experience in school is giving oral presentations or reports. Some students learn rather quickly to alleviate the stress associated with speaking to peers, whereas others require a very controlled and systematic program to develop the abilities necessary to use this study skill effectively. Teacher support and assistance may help to minimize problems related to oral presentations.

Oral presentations may take many forms and may be associated with a variety of subject areas, assignments, or topics. They also may range from reciting a simple sentence to delivering a 15-minute speech. Although the discussion here pertains primarily to oral presentations given in school, the ideas apply to most situations in which students communicate verbally in a formal manner.

One main goal of oral presentations in school is the opportunity for students to learn to communicate to others in an effective, coherent, and organized manner, regardless of the presentation format. For example, such presentations may be made to large or small groups of students, while seated with or standing in front of the group, as individual or group presentations, or as an alternative or accompaniment to completing a written report. They also may include the use of visual aids prepared by the students making the presentations. The development of skills to meet these and similar oral presentation demands requires teacher assistance, as well as continued and regular practice on the part of students.

Elements Related to Oral Presentations

No matter what type of oral presentation is made, students must be prepared. This process includes invoking skills related to (a) knowledge of the presentation topic, (b) the actual delivery of the presentation, and (c) the development and use of support materials and equipment to facilitate a smooth presentation. Specific elements of oral presentations include the following:

- Sufficient knowledge of the topic
- Ability to estimate how the audience members will receive the presentation, including their interest in the topic
- Ensuring that the audience members receive what they perceive to be an interesting and relevant presentation
- Good organization, with smooth transitions from one point to the next
- Appropriate use of visual material and gestures
- Clear and fluent speech, with appropriate emphasis on key words or phrases
- Well-rehearsed presentation prior to actual delivery

As is true of other study skills areas, an interrelationship among study skills is apparent as the elements of oral presentations are examined. Effective notetaking and outlining abilities, report writing, or use of visual aids may contribute to the successful overall delivery of an oral presentation. However, once students have dealt with these other areas, the actual presentation must be made. This section focuses on the delivery itself, whereas more detailed discussions about the other related study skills appear elsewhere in this chapter.

As students prepare for the oral presentation, they must initially ensure that they are sufficiently knowledgeable about the topic. As noted, use of other study skills assists in this knowledge development. Once the topic has been selected and associated research completed, students must focus on (a) identifying components of the presentation, (b) practicing the delivery, and (c) making the actual oral presentation. As they develop oral presentations, speakers should identify

- the main ideas to be addressed,
- related topics to support the main ideas,
- ways to connect the topics during the presentation, and
- the ending for the presentation.

These aspects may be written on cards or in outline form and should represent the basic presentation format.

Once these four elements of the delivery have been identified and fleshed out, students should practice delivering the presentation, using any supporting visual aids. The presentation could be rehearsed with teachers, friends, parents, or siblings at home and should be practiced just the way it will be presented in school. The major purpose of practice deliveries is to work out any potential problems with visual aids, identify areas of strength and weakness, improve on the areas of weakness, practice using note cards if available, practice gestures, and in general build confidence surrounding the presentation.

The actual presentation will be more successful if practiced and rehearsed. The number of rehearsals will vary among students and other circumstances, but students should practice enough times that they feel comfortable and confident with all aspects of the presentation. When making the actual presentation, students should use good eye contact with the audience and deliver the piece the way it was rehearsed, avoiding last-minute major changes.

Identifying Oral Presentation Needs

The Guide for Identifying Oral Presentation Needs (Form 5.18) provides a means for identifying potential problems a student has with oral presentations. Although teachers can often identify these and related indicators of the problems associated with oral presentations, some problems may be detected more accurately through discussions with students. This is especially necessary if teachers wish to fully understand students' feelings and attitudes toward oral presentations. Students who possess adequate abilities in this study skill area may not be entirely free of the anxiety associated with oral presentations; however, they will be able to manage their stress and complete the various procedures outlined above to prepare for the presentation.

The task of making an effective oral presentation requires students to practice and think about their delivery prior to actual implementation. The more prepared students are, the smoother their deliveries. Some level of preparation should occur for any type of oral presentation, no matter how short or long. Knowing the topic in detail, practicing gestures, speaking clearly, and using visual aids appropriately all contribute to effective oral presentations. As a general rule, practice and preparation build confidence in oral presentations, which in turn builds additional confidence for future presentations. The Oral Presentation Guide–Student Form (Form 5.19) provides a guide for students to use as they prepare oral presentations.

Oral Presentations: Best Practices

- Allow extra preparation time for oral presentations, in addition to the time allotted for completion of the written report.

- Provide a nonthreatening environment for oral presentations to reduce peer criticism.

- Be flexible in structuring the conditions in which students make oral presentations (e.g., seated in or standing by their desks, in front of a small group, in front of the whole class).

- Instruct students to make oral presentations in different situations (e.g., one-on-one, small group, whole class).

- Provide students with an outline of a topic and instruct them to provide a written or oral narrative summary of the ideas covered therein.

- Provide opportunities for students to share information orally through various methods (e.g., debates, interviews, investigative reporting).

Guide for Identifying Oral Presentation Needs

Student Name _____

Completed by _____ Date _____

Directions: Check the box next to each behavior that the student exhibits on a regular and consistent basis. Summarize the areas of need to complete the guide.

☐ Demonstrates unusual fear about giving oral presentations

☐ Does not use visual aids effectively during oral presentations

☐ Lacks sufficient preparation for oral presentations

☐ Lacks sufficient knowledge about the topics presented during oral presentations

☐ Is generally unwilling to participate freely in oral presentations

☐ Has difficulty speaking clearly during presentations but not during other types of verbal interactions

☐ Cannot accurately read the audience of an oral presentation

☐ Does not use gestures effectively during oral presentations

☐ Is unable to organize the content in oral presentations

☐ Has difficulty making clear transitions during oral presentations

☐ Is unable to make oral presentations from an outline, note cards, or memory

☐ Has difficulty understanding the purposes of oral presentations

Summary comments: _____

_____

_____

_____

Oral Presentation Guide—Student Form

Student _____ Date _____

Title of presentation _____

Length of presentation _____

Directions: Check each item if it reflects your oral presentation. This should be completed before and after the oral presentation.

- ☐ Is the presentation organized?
- ☐ Is the presentation rehearsed sufficiently?
- ☐ Do you understand what the audience should get out of the presentation?
- ☐ Is the introduction to the presentation clear and well rehearsed?
- ☐ Are concluding statements clear and well rehearsed?
- ☐ Is necessary visual material prepared?
- ☐ Do you understand when and how to use the developed visuals?
- ☐ Have you considered where to position yourself in the room during the presentation?
- ☐ Do you understand the purpose of the presentation?
- ☐ Have you anticipated various questions from the audience?
- ☐ Do you know the topic in sufficient detail to feel comfortable responding to anticipated questions?
- ☐ Do you feel comfortable with the planned delivery of the presentation?

Opportunities to Learn

Time Management: Making Good Use of Time

The critical elements of this study skill are

- Organizing daily and weekly activities
- Prioritizing activities
- Completing tasks on time
- Reorganizing time as necessary

Importance of Time Management in School

Even the most well-organized students may become easily frustrated with the seemingly endless amount of work and requirements demanded of them in school. In addition to expecting assignments to be completed in a timely manner, teachers often demand high-quality work from students. Meanwhile, many students pursue extracurricular interests and activities. Effective time management helps students to complete requirements and other tasks in an efficient and timely manner.

Time management serves several important functions, including helping students to

- Organize and budget their use of time effectively
- Determine how accurate they were in keeping projected timelines and schedules
- Complete tasks within required time limits
- Minimize wasted time used to complete activities
- Meet individual recreational or leisure-time goals
- Acquire and maintain control over their use of time
- Complete required tasks more quickly and accurately, resulting in more time available to engage in recreational activities of their choice
- Prioritize activities to ensure that the appropriate amounts of time (neither too much nor too little) are spent on various tasks, activities, or requirements

In short, effective time management provides students with a greater sense of ownership and control over their own lives as they meet academic, social, and personal demands. It may help students feel greater self-satisfaction with their own accomplishments, whether completed for themselves or to meet school requirements.

Elements Related to Time Management

Several steps constitute effective time management:

1. Identify tasks to complete.
2. Prioritize tasks or goals, considering importance, extent, and time constraints.
3. Develop a schedule to complete tasks or goals in the order of priority.
4. Work toward meeting established timelines while monitoring progress.
5. Review the projected timelines for meeting goals or completing tasks to determine accuracy of the projections.
6. Adjust future time management schedules and priorities based on past performance and reviews of previous time management schedules.

The first step in determining and budgeting time is to document the tasks or goals to address. Timelines may include daily, weekly, monthly, or semester schedules. Effective time managers establish semester and monthly schedules and then generate weekly and daily schedules to assist in meeting the longer term goals. For example, once a learner knows the major requirements in school for a semester or a month, he or she should record these to show exact dates due. Weekly schedules should reflect specific timelines associated with each week in the monthly schedule, whereas daily schedules should reflect the weekly deadlines. Thus, daily schedules assist in meeting weekly schedules, and these in turn help to meet the monthly or semester schedules. Although not all semester or monthly requirements are known at the beginning of each time period, those that are can be easily included in a long-term schedule of deadlines. However, monthly and semester schedules must be revised as periodic additions arise. As tasks or goals are documented, they form the basis for developing appropriate time management schedules to meet daily, weekly, monthly, or semester requirements.

After listing the various goals or tasks and their due dates, students need to prioritize the order in which to address these items. The students need to consider the importance of each task, its complexity, the amount of time required to complete it, and the exact date when the task or goal must be completed. From this information, the students can begin to form their semester, monthly, weekly, and daily schedules. When and where each task falls in the daily or weekly schedules depend on the due date and the estimated time required to complete the task. To the extent possible, similar tasks should be completed at the same time to minimize duplicating efforts.

Semester or monthly schedules can be documented easily on a calendar to show when various tasks or goals should be completed. Weekly schedules present more specific breakdowns of monthly schedules and should be completed at or near the beginning of each week. Daily time management schedules break down the weekly schedules and should be completed prior to beginning the day's activities. Students should be taught that the purpose for developing these different schedules is to help them know when to begin tasks to meet their goals or requirements, as well as when these must be completed.

Students should attempt to complete as many of the tasks outlined on the daily schedules as possible. They should record when they begin and complete each task to help them evaluate the accuracy of their projections for task completion. Students should review their completed schedules and adjust future daily or weekly schedules accordingly (e.g., allow more time for certain types of activities, begin certain tasks earlier, allow less time for certain types of tasks). Through this systematic planning, scheduling, and reviewing of schedules, students can develop and maintain effective time management study skills abilities.

Identifying Time Management Needs

Time management problems may be evident when a student does not complete work on time as well as when the quality of work submitted is substandard. Effective time management also requires meeting personal, school, and home requirements or goals. Meeting only imposed requirements and not personal goals may pose problems to some students, as a balance between the two should be maintained. Effective time managers are able to find this balance in their lives. They can develop time schedules, accurately project required time allotments, keep within established time schedules, and spend quality time engaged in various activities while minimizing wasted time.

Students must continually strive to find the balance between time allotted for required tasks and recreational or leisure activities. Effective time management requires knowing when not to spend time on an activity or task as well as when to spend extra time on it. Regular teacher–student interactions concerning the development of time management schedules help students to assume responsibility for their own time. The few minutes a day and several minutes each week spent developing and reviewing time management schedules may save students from an enormous amount of wasted time and increase their time available for recreational, leisure, and family activities. Students who have difficulty managing their time effectively may exhibit a variety of behaviors. Indicators of potential problems associated with effective time management are addressed on the Guide for Identifying Time Management Needs (Form 5.20).

The monthly and daily time management schedules for students (Forms 5.21 and 5.22) should be completed once all or most of the required activities have been identified. Longer term schedules may be developed easily using a monthly calendar or Form 5.21 to document various deadlines. When monthly requirements have been identified, daily tasks should be documented using Form 5.22. Once the daily activities have been identified, they should be categorized into primary and secondary tasks. Primary tasks are those that must be completed that day; secondary tasks are activities students would like to address but could attend to on a different day if necessary.

After prioritizing tasks into primary and secondary categories on Form 5.22, students document the estimated amount of time they believe necessary to complete each task and the time during the day when each task will be addressed (e.g., during study hall, after recess, at 4:00 P.M.). If the task is attempted that day, the student records the times at which work started and ended, as well as the time spent on the task.

Once all this information has been recorded, students and teachers can see which primary and secondary tasks were attempted, the time estimated versus the time required, and the time of day the tasks were completed compared to when the students initially planned to address them. Effective time managers accurately estimate the time required to complete tasks, address the primary tasks when necessary, and complete the tasks at or near the time of day projected when the daily schedule was developed. Adjustments to subsequent daily schedules should be made if students are not accurately estimating required time allotments or the time of day to address the task. Completion and use of this type of daily time management schedule help students to manage their time more efficiently, which in turn minimizes wasted time and increases on-time completion of daily, weekly, monthly, and semester assignments.

Time Management: Best Practices

- Provide students with specific opportunities during which they are required to budget their own time.

- Verbally encourage on-task behaviors, especially during independent work times.

- Ensure that students know the allotted time for completion of each activity.

- Provide sufficient opportunity for students to manage their time and complete assigned tasks.

- Assign a group of students a task. Instruct students to discuss how they will budget their time to complete the task.

- Instruct students to estimate the amount of time required to complete a task and then record the actual amount of time it takes. Compare the results.

- Instruct students to record how their time is spent outside of school. Discuss the distribution of time with them.

- Instruct students to keep a notebook with daily assignments and due dates.

- Instruct students to construct a semester calendar, including various dates for tests, papers, and events.

- Suggest that students set a timer prior to beginning assigned tasks. Have them record the number of activities completed within the self-allotted time, along with the actual time required to complete the tasks. Students may also time their work on one specific task.

- Instruct students to list and prioritize daily or weekly activities. Have them record the order in which they are actually completed, and compare results.

- Allow students opportunities to share their time management procedures with other classmates.

- Reward students for effective use of time.

Guide for Identifying Time Management Needs

Student Name _____

Completed by _____ Date _____

Directions: Check the box next to each behavior that the student exhibits on a regular and consistent basis. Summarize the areas of need to complete the guide.

☐ Is unable to complete tasks at school on time

☐ Completes tasks on time but with sloppy or unorganized appearance

☐ Submits work on time, but it lacks sufficient details to be complete

☐ Is unable to develop time schedules

☐ Is unable to keep to developed time schedules

☐ Cannot organize daily activities

☐ Demonstrates little understanding of the importance of time management

☐ Is unable to reorganize time to meet last-minute demands

☐ Is unable to keep scheduled timelines to meet personal or recreational goals, even though deadlines are met at school

☐ Does not learn from previous time-management errors

☐ Does not accept responsibility for own time management

☐ Takes unusually long periods of time to complete even simple tasks

Summary comments: _____

_____

_____

_____

Monthly Time Management Schedule—Student Form

Name _____ Month/year _____ / _____

SUN	MON	TUE	WED	THU	FRI	SAT

Daily Time Management Form

Name _____ Date _____

Primary Tasks	Estimated Time to Complete Task	Time of Day to Complete Task	Time Task Began/ Completed	Actual Time to Complete Task

(continues)

FORM 5.22 Continued.

Daily Time Management Form

Name _____

Date _____

Secondary Tasks	Estimated Time to Complete Task	Time of Day to Complete Task	Time Task Began/ Completed	Actual Time to Complete Task

Self-Management: Managing Own Behaviors

The critical elements of this study skill are

- Monitoring and regulating one's own behavior
- Assuming responsibility for one's own actions
- Changing one's behavior as necessary

Importance of Self-Management in School

In addition to time management, many students must also learn to manage their own behavior, especially during independent work time. Inappropriate behaviors can interfere seriously with task completion, even though a student possesses sufficient study skills in other areas.

Programs emphasizing self-management and control of behavior assist students in assuming responsibility for their own behaviors, and becoming aware of one's behavior is often sufficient impetus to improve or change it (Brown, 2004). Self-management helps students mediate their own behaviors and is an effective technique for reducing the time required for task completion. Self-monitoring also helps reduce demands placed on teachers by reducing data collection responsibilities (Lewis & Doorlag, 2002). Although self-management is important to facilitate learning, many students with learning disabilities experience difficulties monitoring their work or progress toward stated goals. As a result, self-management skills should be included in the total study skills program, as they are effective skills for helping students to monitor their own behaviors and change those behaviors that interfere with the completion of assigned tasks.

Elements Related to Self-Management

Effective self-management requires

- ability to evaluate one's own behavior,
- easy-to-implement self-monitoring procedures, and
- consistent self-reinforcement of appropriate behavior.

In addition, teacher support in student self-management is very important. As students begin their self-management program, teachers should observe and interview them to determine their current levels of abilities in addressing these three elements. Students must also possess a certain level of motivation to want to address and change their own behaviors. Furthermore, related skills such as the ability to anticipate consequences, manage frustration, and appreciate feelings are important factors in effective self-management (Fagen, Long, & Stevens, 1975).

Identifying Self-Management Needs

The Guide for Identifying Self-Management Needs (Form 5.23) provides an informal means of identifying self-management needs. These indicators assist both students and teachers in planning a self-management program. Students who experience difficulties with monitoring their own behaviors, assuming responsibilities for their behaviors, changing behaviors on their own, and being distracted during independent, small-group, or whole-class work times exhibit behaviors that indicate a need for more effective self-management. Through skills related to self-monitoring, self-instruction, self-correction, and problem solving, students may better assess and remediate off-task behaviors with a minimum amount of direct teacher intervention.

Self-Management: Best Practices

- Ensure that students are aware of specific behavioral expectations when completing specific tasks.
- Monitor self-management programs and progress with students.
- Assist students in setting realistic and attainable goals in their self-management programs.
- Be consistent in the implementation of behavioral expectations.
- Instruct students to develop a self-monitoring chart concerning a selected behavior and to record a check each time the behavior is exhibited. Review results with each student.
- Provide students an alternative place in the classroom to complete their work. Allow them the freedom to choose the place to work.
- Complete a contract with a student outlining the timelines, procedures, and rewards for completing work (Brown, 2004).
- Provide students with activities for evaluating consequences prior to the action (e.g., specify what might happen as a result of a particular behavior).
- Role-play situations that contain several possible solutions and discuss the implications of each.
- Provide students with opportunities to distinguish thoughts from actions. For example, allow students to respond to the question, "Have you ever thought about doing something but decided not to?" Explore reasons why it was a good idea not to engage in the activity.

Guide for Identifying Self-Management Needs

Student Name _____

Completed by _____ Date _____

Directions: Check the box next to each behavior that the student exhibits on a regular and consistent basis. Summarize the areas of need to complete the guide.

☐ Seems unaware of specific behavioral expectations when completing tasks

☐ Has difficulty establishing realistic and attainable goals

☐ Is unable to monitor own behaviors

☐ Does not assume responsibility for own behaviors

☐ Refuses to change own behaviors without direct teacher intervention

☐ Displays inappropriate behaviors that interfere with task completion

☐ Spends limited time on task during independent work times

☐ Is easily distracted during small-group work

☐ Is easily distracted during whole class activities

☐ Is unable to see the relationship between off-task behaviors and incomplete or late assignments

☐ Is unable to maintain a consistent work pattern to complete assigned tasks

Summary comments: _____

_____

_____

_____

Organization: Managing Learning-Related Activities

The critical elements related to this study skill are

- Organizing key demands of everyday school life
- Organizing key home-focused activities associated with school
- Managing personal organizational demands

Importance of Organizational Skills in School

Some level of organizational competence is required to be successful in schools today. It helps with other study skills, including time management, note taking, report writing, and test taking. Organizational abilities are also needed at home because much school-related behavior occurs at home in the evenings or over the weekend in the form of homework and other assigned projects. Organizational skills also benefit one's personal life, as displaying good organization in personal matters indirectly affects school-related issues. For example, having the bathroom organized facilitates getting ready in the morning and helps one to be on time. Although organizational skills may seem related to an innate ability in individuals, they really are skills that can be learned. For some individuals, however, creative compensatory techniques may be the more suitable choice.

As student expectations continue to increase in schools, additional pressure is placed on learners to (a) complete more work in shorter amounts of time, (b) achieve higher proficiency levels in the work they do, and (c) become more independent and self-directed with a variety of learning-related tasks as they get older. Accordingly, the independent implementation of organizational demands increases with age. A certain amount of organizational assistance is provided to young students by their teachers and parents; however, as students move to the upper elementary level, they need more self-direction in the area of organizational skills. As educational demands increase, students either succeed in handling the daily challenges they face in school and at home or they become increasingly frustrated unless they possess effective and efficient organizational skills.

Students must be able to maneuver the demands of school and home in terms of organization. They must understand learning tasks and timelines to make informed decisions as to how and in what order they must organize their learning. Abilities to organize and manage classroom learning and associated tasks, which typically require efficient and effective organizational skills, are critical in today's schools, especially for those who have learning problems. The fact that learning-related tasks carry over to home (e.g., homework) underscores the importance of these skills.

The consequences of not being organized include a range of undesirable outcomes. Student are apt to turn in homework late or not at all; fail to complete assignments as directed; waste excessive amounts of time looking for things; be late for class (i.e., accumulate excessive numbers of tardy citations); miss key deadlines; receive failing grades; and become very frustrated with themselves and others. All of these outcomes can be avoided or, at the very least, minimized by teaching students useful organizational skills.

Organizational skills that students need to learn include the following:

- Having books, supplies, and other materials organized for quick retrieval and usage at school, particularly at the secondary level where students are assigned lockers and have little time between classes

- Using backpacks or other means for carrying essential books and materials to and from school

- Managing the significant amounts of paper (e.g., lecture notes, handouts, forms)

- Creating and maintaining an effective place for homework

- Developing storage systems at home for easy access to important documents and resource materials

- Effectively organizing one's personal life

- Being able to manage multiple tasks and assignments

- Effectively using two or more study skills simultaneously

Overall, use of organizational skills assists students with learning problems to more effectively manage their own learning, especially when less teacher direction is provided. Students who organize themselves with the long-term goal of completing tasks within established timelines will be more successful in school and better able to enjoy their personal and leisure time.

Elements Related to Organizational Skills

Students need to learn effective use of organizational skills related to the following activities:

Everyday School Activities
- Locker usage

- Backpack or other transport equipment usage

- Supplies management

- In-school document and paper management

- Use of multiple study skills

School-Related Activities at Home
- Maintenance of study area or bedroom

- Maintenance of desk and storage areas

Personal-Level Activities
- Managing personal effects

- Organizing time to manage multiple tasks

Initial organizational efforts by students should focus on simple methods and strategies for managing their own learning. As mentioned previously, in the early elementary grades, teachers provide a certain level of organization. Interestingly, more secondary-level teachers are now requiring specific school supplies (e.g., 2-inch binder, accordian folders) for their classes in an effort to maximize organizational effectiveness. Some schools or teachers provide to their students preprinted planners that include key events and important dates. All of these efforts assist students in dealing with the organizational demands of school. Ultimately, however, the extent of organizational depth (i.e., how much structure is necessary) and organizational support (i.e., how much assistance is needed from others) required will depend on the student.

Unfortunately, the more teachers provide directions to assist students with the organizational demands of school, the less students need to generate and direct their own organizational skills activity. To best prepare students with learning problems to acquire, maintain, and generalize organizational skills, teachers should gradually introduce more independence in student learning and assist with transitions to less teacher-directed activities. Teachers should provide time for students to schedule and organize their learning and give students feedback on how well they adhered to their own organization. In addition, promoting self-monitoring by learners is a highly effective strategy for helping students acquire and maintain organizational skills.

Although organization is a task within itself, effective organization involves the simultaneous application and usage of other study skills. For example, effective test-taking skills inherently include efficient organization. Additionally, skills in notetaking and outlining, library usage, and use of reference materials help students organize their work when completing research projects and similar assignments. As students with learning or behavior problems attempt to deal with multiple tasks leading to several different assignments over a defined period of time (e.g., a school week), time management and self-management study skills become increasingly important.

Identifying Organization Needs

Strengths and weaknesses associated with organizational abilities are easily observed in classroom tasks. Effective organizational skills are evident when students demonstrate the following within a classroom:

- Efficiency in task completion
- Proficiency in task completion
- Ability to manage several tasks or learning concepts simultaneously
- Ability to employ multiple study skills to complete assignments

Students who possess adequate organizational skills are not intimidated by multiple assignments with varying expectations of proficiency. They also do not become easily confused as expectations for self-organization are introduced in the learning environment. The Guide for Identifying Organization Needs (Form 5.24) addresses potential problems with organizational skills.

Organization: Suggested Practices

The suggested practices for helping students develop organizational skills are divided into four areas: general suggestions, school-focused suggestions, home suggestions, and personal-level suggestions.

General Suggestions
- Emphasize the importance of organizing one's own learning.
- Provide systematic opportunities in the classroom for student-directed learning.
- Develop with the student a self-organization plan, emphasizing the order for multiple task completion, timelines for completing each task separately and all tasks collectively, and measures for determining student success with the organizational plan.
- Provide students with the opportunity to self-monitor their own organization.

- Provide students with three interrelated tasks and instruct them to generate a plan to successfully manage completion of all tasks within required timelines.
- Initiate fewer teacher-directed tasks and assist students to use cooperative learning techniques to organize and complete assignments in small groups.
- Provide students with activities in which organization is central to successful completion.
- Allow students the opportunity to share their organizational strategies with others in the classroom.
- Instruct students to keep a daily log of how they organized their daily activities at school and home and to evaluate the implementation of that organization.

School-Focused Suggestions
- With the help of parents, examine ways to organize students' lockers using shelves, hooks, and magnetized items (e.g., writing surfaces). Items to "accessorize" one's locker (Goldberg & Zwiebel, 2005) can be purchased in office supply and other types of stores. For students who have more than one locker (e.g., school and dance class), this suggestion applies to all locker situations.
- Encourage students to keep backup supplies in their lockers (e.g., extra paper, writing instruments, batteries for calculators or cell phones, tissues, and a small amount of money for lunch or emergencies).
- With the help of parents and in consideration of the personal desires of the student, select a backpack that allows for effective organization of school items and personal effects. (Some backpacks are definitely better than others for organizing.)
- Help each student determine a way to manage homework assignments that fits his or her personal lifestyle.
- List important items (e.g., books, binders, other supplies) that students need for each class and post this on locker doors or insert in planners or other personal items that students carry. This list can be input into a personal digital assistant (PDA).
- If a specific class does not require the use of some type of binder system, consider using one to help students organize papers and other documents during the school day.
- Provide students with sufficient opportunities to organize their own time and to implement that organization.
- Ensure that students are aware of the different ways in which various study skills can be used together to better manage learning.
- Provide pairs of students with a situation in which they are required to meet established proficiency levels while meeting established timelines. Instruct them to develop a plan for ensuring that they meet both proficiency levels and time limits.

Home Suggestions
- It is important to create a work area where the student will do his or her homework. This area should be cleared of most items and have a designated place for the student to put his or her backpack.
- A desk of some type is the preferred location for students to do their homework. The desk must be organized so that a student can efficiently do his or her homework. Work space on the desk may need to be organized around a computer, if one is available. Many homework activities require a flat, clear surface

that allows enough space to spread out materials. If the desk does not provide enough space for some tasks, the student may need to use a table surface.

- Students need to have storage areas for textbooks, other course-related books (e.g., novels), reference materials (e.g., Spanish/English dictionary), course-related papers and documents, technological devices (e.g., calculator), and office supplies. The extent of structure needed depends on the student. For instance, some students use desk drawers with organizing trays to help keep things in order.

- The use of filing systems may be helpful. Expanding files or other similar systems can be useful.

- Parents can help students rearrange their bedrooms to fit the "kindergarten model of organization." According to Morgenstern (1998), this model is based on the following observation: "Walk into any kindergarten classroom in the world, and you will behold the perfect model of organization" (p. 50). It is based on the following principles: (a) The room is divided into activity zones; (b) it is easy to focus on one activity at a time; (c) items are stored at their point of use; (d) it is fun to put things away—everything has a home; and (e) everything that is important is shown on a visual menu.

Personal-Level Suggestions

- Students should use a well-designed, print-based planner or PDA to help them manage the multiple tasks that occur in a day, week, month, grading period, semester, or year.

- All systems used for organization at school and at home should be reexamined regularly to clear out materials that are not needed and to update the organization based on current needs.

- Organizing various areas at home, such as the bathroom and the student's closet, will help him or her get ready for school in the morning or the night before. Accessories devised to improve home organization can be purchased from many stores.

- Apply the following needs assessment questions (Morgenstern, 1998) to help identify and address organizational problems.

  What is working?

  What is not working?

  What items and outcomes are most essential to you?

  Why do you want to get organized?

  What is causing the problem?

Guide for Identifying Organization Needs

Student Name _____

Completed by _____ Date _____

Directions: Check the box next to each behavior that the student exhibits on a regular and consistent basis. Summarize the areas of need to complete the guide.

☐ Is unable to keep locker orderly, resulting in items being misplaced or lost and delays in getting required items

☐ Does not transport school-related items to and from school effectively and efficiently

☐ Is unable to bring the appropriate materials needed for class

☐ Loses or misplaces papers and other documents that are distributed in class or at school

☐ Is unable to successfully employ multiple study skills to meet multiple classroom demands

☐ Is unable to create a study area at home that is conducive to completing homework or other assigned projects

☐ Cannot keep the desk uncluttered

☐ Is unable to create and effectively use storage areas near the work area

☐ Cannot manage multiple tasks or learning-related activities due to disorganization

☐ Is unable to adjust organization of multiple tasks after repreated failures

☐ Lacks understanding of the importance of effective organization of one's tasks

Summary comments: _____

_____

_____

_____

Structured Study and Learning Strategies: A Potpourri of Formalized Techniques

The effective use of structured study and learning strategies facilitates greater academic achievement and social success.

This chapter presents a variety of structured learning and study strategies that students may use to address their needs. These strategies facilitate better task completion and retention of information while helping students to become more independent learners.

Learning Strategies

Specific classroom-level efforts to address students' various learning and study styles may be implemented through use of learning strategies. The primary purpose of learning strategies is to assist students to gain greater control over their learning and increase their capacity to learn. Effectively meeting diverse needs in the classroom necessitates student acquisition mastery and appropriate implementation of learning strategies. As students become more proficient with learning strategies within an overall study skills program, effective accommodations to learning may best occur. Various learning strategies are discussed by numerous researchers (Bender, 2002; Hoover, 2001; Hoover & Collier, 2003; Hoover & Patton, 2005; Marks, Laeys, Bender, & Scott, 1998; Mastropieri & Scruggs, 1998). This chapter presents and discusses six broadly defined learning strategies that complement and support student learning in a comprehensive study skills and study strategies program. Each learning strategy is defined briefly. A form is provided at the end of the chapter for each learning strategy to help students successfully apply these strategies in the classroom. These forms were developed from information found in the previously listed sources.

Active processing strategies facilitate self-talk or self-questioning for the purpose of activating prior knowledge related to the content being studied. Strategies that require the learner to use questions to scan, summarize, question, and predict activate prior knowledge and generate the use of the active processing learning strategy. (See Form 6.1 at the end of this chapter.)

Analogy strategies facilitate student recall of previously learned content and information relevant to the topic being studied. Strategies that require the learner to use schema, cloze, and metaphor procedures reflect the classroom application of the analogy learning strategy. (See Form 6.2.)

Rehearsal strategies facilitate student reflection on a task prior to, during, and after its completion. Rehearsals allow students to think through what they are doing as they complete a task. Strategies that require the learner to review, recite, and recall different aspects related to the tasks reflect the classroom application of the rehearsal learning strategy. (See Form 6.3.)

Coping strategies facilitate an objective and systematic process for addressing tasks. Coping allows students to confront issues related to tasks in an organized and structured problem-solving manner. Strategies that require the learner to confront issues, develop solutions, identify necessary assistance, attempt solutions, and persist until task completion reflect the classroom application of the coping learning strategy. (See Form 6.4.)

‖ **Evaluation** strategies facilitate student awareness of what must be done to successfully complete a task. Evaluation also allows students to know when they have successfully completed the task through ongoing monitoring. Strategies that require the learner to self-monitor, self-check, predict, and generalize reflect the classroom application of the evaluation learning strategy. (See Form 6.5.)

‖ **Organization** strategies facilitate student grouping or clustering of ideas, tasks, and skills. Organization allows students to categorize and group ideas and skills in a way that will provide structure for successful task completion. Strategies that require the learner to look for and use patterns, classify information into various groupings, and break down information into manageable units reflect the classroom application of the organization learning strategy. (See Form 6.6.)

Processes for selecting and using learning strategies have been discussed by various authors (Bender, 2002; Day & Elksnin, 1994; Hoover & Patton, 2005) and include the following suggestions:

1. Match the selected strategies to the task or particular setting in which the student is working.
2. Determine the student's current level of ability and knowledge of the strategy prior to using the strategy.
3. Teach, review, and model the learning strategy while providing specific examples.
4. Provide guided practice and encourage the students to verbalize the steps within the learning strategy.
5. Employ use of the strategy in assigned classroom tasks or facilitate self-management of behavior.
6. Monitor and evaluate the effectiveness of the learning strategy on content and performance knowledge and skills.

Study Strategies

High-quality teachers are able to implement a study skills program on a regular and consistent basis by helping students learn to successfully apply procedures associated with different study strategies. Table 6.1 lists numerous study strategies available to teachers and students to successfully learn. The table provides overview information regarding each selected strategy, including the task areas emphasized through use of the strategy, the general process associated with the strategy, and comments related to the classroom use of the strategy. These are some of the frequently discussed structured study strategies; the list is not all-inclusive. Although not all strategies are appropriate for use in all class settings or for all students, these selections represent techniques that may prove effective to meet some students' needs. In developing this table, we used information found in a variety of sources (Bos & Vaughn, 2006; Czarnecki, Rosko, & Pine, 1998; de la Paz, 1997; Heaton & O'Shea, 1995; Hoover, 2004b; Hoover & Patton, 2005; Ogle, 1986).

Table 6.1
Study Strategies

Strategy	Task Area	Process	Description
CALL-UP	Notetaking	**C**opy ideas accurately **A**dd necessary details **L**isten and write the question **L**isten and write the answer **U**se text to support notes **P**ut response in own words	Helps students to remain focused on what is happening in class during a notetaking task or assignment; helps learners respond more accurately to questions using notes and text to support written responses (Czarnecki, Rosko, & Pine, 1998)
CAN-DO	Acquiring content	**C**reate list of items to learn **A**sk self if list is complete **N**ote details and main ideas **D**escribe components and their relationships **O**verlearn main items, followed by learning details	Assists with memorization of lists of items through rehearsal techniques
COPS	Written reports	**C**apitalization correct **O**verall appearance **P**unctuation correct **S**pelling correct	Provides a structure for proofreading written work prior to submitting it to the teacher
DEFENDS	Written expression	**D**ecide on a specific position **E**xamine own reasons for this position **F**orm a list of points explaining each reason **E**xpose position in first sentence of written task **N**ote each reason and associated points **D**rive home position in last sentence **S**earch for and correct any errors	Helps learners defend a particular position in a written assignment
EASY	Studying content	**E**licit questions (*who, what when, where, why*) **A**sk self which information is least difficult **S**tudy easy content initially, followed by difficult content **Y**es—provide self-reinforcement	Helps learners organize and prioritize information by responding to questions designed to identify important content to be learned
FIST	Reading comprehension	**F**irst sentence is read **I**ndicate a question based on material in first sentence **S**earch for answer to question **T**ie question and answer together through paraphrasing	Helps students actively pursue responses to questions related directly to material being read
GLP	Notetaking	**G**uided **L**ecture **P**rocedure	Provides students with a structure for taking notes during lectures; uses group activity to facilitate effective notetaking

(continues)

Table 6.1 *Continued.*
Study Strategies

Strategy	Task Area	Process	Description
KWL	Reading comprehension	**K**now—document what you know **W**ant to know—document what you want to know **L**earn—list what you have learned	Helps students with reading comprehension and organization of their thoughts, ideas, and acquired knowledge by relating previous knowledge with desired learning (Ogle, 1986)
MARKER	Time management Organization	**M**ake a list of goals, set the order, set the date **A**rrange a plan for each goal and predict your success **R**un your plans for each goal and adjust if necessary **K**eep records of your progress **E**valuate your progress toward each goal **R**eward yourself when you reach a goal and set a new goal	Helps students effectively use their time by staying focused on their goals and to reward themselves when goal has been reached (Bos & Vaughn, 2006)
NEAT	Writing	**N**ever hand in messy work **E**very paper should be readable **A**lways keep your paper clean **T**ry to remember to put your name and the date on every paper	Assists students to double-check their written work for neatness prior to submission
Panorama	Reading	Preparatory stage—identify purpose Intermediate stage—survey and read Concluding stage—memorize material	Includes a three-stage process to assist with reading comprehension
PARS	Reading	**P**review **A**sk questions **R**ead **S**ummarize	Is used with younger students and with those who have limited experiences with study strategies
PENS	Sentence writing	**P**ick a formula **E**xplore different words to fit into the formula **N**ote the words selected **S**ubject and verb selections follow	Is appropriate for developing basic sentence structure and helps students write different types of sentences by following formulas for sentence construction
PIRATES	Test taking	**P**repare to succeed **I**nspect instructions carefully **R**ead entire question, remember memory strategies, and reduce choices **A**nswer question or leave until later **T**urn back to the abandoned items **E**stimate unknown answers by avoiding absolutes and eliminating similar choices **S**urvey to ensure that all items have a response	Helps learners to complete tests more carefully and successfully

(continues)

Structured Study and Learning Strategies

133

Table 6.1 *Continued.*
Study Strategies

Strategy	Task Area	Process	Description
PQ4R	Reading	**P**review **Q**uestion **R**ead **R**eflect **R**ecite **R**eview	Helps students to become more discriminating readers
5Rs	Test taking	**R**ecord—take notes on right side of paper **R**educe—write in key words, phrases, and questions on left side of paper **R**ecite—talk aloud **R**eflect—question how this relates to what you know **R**eview—read over notes and summarize at bottom of page	Helps students to prepare to take tests; helps students clarify and reflect on what they know and how knowledge relates to potential test items
RAP	Reading comprehension	**R**ead paragraph **A**sk self to identify the main idea and two supporting details **P**ut main idea and details into own words	Helps students to learn information through paraphrasing
RARE	Reading	**R**eview selection questions **A**nswer all questions known **R**ead the selection **E**xpress answers to remaining questions	Emphasizes reading for a specific purpose while focusing on acquiring answers to selection questions initially not known
RDPE	Underlining	**R**eview entire passage **D**ecide which ideas are important **P**lan the underlining to include only main points **E**valuate results of the underlining by reading only the underlined words	Helps learners organize and remember main points and ideas in a reading selection through appropriate underlining of key words
REAP	Reading Writing Thinking	**R**ead **E**ncode **A**nnotate **P**onder	Helps students combine several skills to facilitate discussion about reading material
ReQuest	Reading Questioning	**Re**ciprocal **Quest**ioning	Helps students to model teacher questions and receive feedback while exploring the meaning of the reading material
RIDER	Reading comprehension	**R**ead sentence **I**mage (form mental picture) **D**escribe how new image differs from previous sentence **E**valuate image to ensure that it contains all necessary elements **R**epeat process with subsequent sentences	Cues the learner to form a mental image of what was previously learned from a sentence just read

(continues)

Table 6.1 *Continued.*
Study Strategies

Strategy	Task Area	Process	Description
SCORER	Test taking	**S**chedule time effectively **C**lue words identified **O**mit difficult items until end **R**ead carefully **E**stimate answers requiring calculations **R**eview work and responses	Provides a structure for completing various tests by helping students carefully and systematically complete test items
SOLVE IT	Math word problems	**S**ay the problem to yourself **O**mit any unnecessary information in problem **L**isten for key vocabulary terms or indicators **V**ocabulary—change to fit math concepts **E**quation—translate problem into a math equation **I**ndicate the answer **T**ranslate answer back into context of word problem	Assists students to systematically solve math word problems by focusing on key vocabulary in the problem and relating the terms to math concepts and solutions
SQRQCQ	Math word problems	**S**urvey word problem **Q**uestion asked is identified **R**ead more carefully **Q**uestion process required to solve problem **C**ompute the answer **Q**uestion self to ensure that the answer solves the problem	Provides a systematic structure for identifying the question being asked in a math word problem, computing the response, and ensuring that the question in the problem was answered
SQ3R	Reading	**S**urvey **Q**uestion **R**ead **R**ecite **R**eview	Provides a systematic approach to improve reading comprehension
SSCD	Vocabulary development	**S**ound clues used **S**tructure clues used **C**ontext clues used **D**ictionary used	Encourages students to remember to use sound, structure, and context clues, as well as a dictionary if needed, to address unfamiliar vocabulary
STOP	Writing	**S**uspend judgment (brainstorm) **T**ell thesis **O**rganize ideas **P**lan moves for effective writing	Helps students remember to brainstorm to document potential ideas, generate a thesis statement, document main and subordinate ideas in outline form, and plan for effective writing (de la Paz, 1997)
TOWER	Written reports Organization	**T**hink **O**rder ideas **W**rite **E**dit **R**ewrite	Provides a structure for completing initial and final drafts of written reports; may be used effectively with COPS

(continues)

Structured Study and Learning Strategies

Table 6.1 *Continued.*
Study Strategies

Strategy	Task Area	Process	Description
TQLR	Listening	**T**uning in **Q**uestioning **L**istening **R**eviewing	Assists with listening comprehension by reminding students to generate questions and listen for specific statements related to those questions

Guide to Using Active Processing Strategies

Name _____ Date _____

Goal/Task _____

Directions: For each step, write questions in your own words or draw a picture to help you recall what to do to achieve the goal or task.

1. Define the goal or task you wish to achieve.

2. List the steps to follow in order to achieve the goal or task.

3. Evaluate your work. Check your answers.

4. Try a different approach if something does not work.

5. Know that the task is complete.

Guide to Using Analogy Strategies

Name _____ Date _____

Item/topic of study _____

Directions: For each step, write statements in your own words or draw a picture to help you recall things you already know about the specific topic or item you are studying.

1. Some things that I know that are like the new item/topic:

2. How the new item/topic compares to the items I listed above:

3. Other items that might be used instead of the new item:

4. Some of my prior experiences or knowledge that I could use as examples to show that I understand the new item/topic:

Guide to Using Rehearsal Strategies

Name _____ Date _____

Topic _____

Directions: For each step, write a statement in your own words or draw a picture to help you review and recall what you have just seen or heard about a topic you are studying.

1. What I have just seen or heard:

2. Questions that I will ask myself to help remember what I have seen or heard:

3. The mental picture that I am making about what I have seen or heard:

4. A summary of what I have seen or heard related to the topic includes these points:

Guide to Using Coping Strategies

Name _____ Date _____

Problem _____

Directions: For each step, write a statement in your own words or draw a picture to help you solve the problem.

1. The problem can be broken into the following parts:

2. The order in which I should address the parts:

3. One solution to address each part:

4. The help I need to address the problem:

5. When I will know that I am ready to begin to solve the problem:

6. Other solutions I can try to solve the problem if those I choose do not work:

7. When I will know that my problem is solved:

Guide to Using Evaluation Strategies

Name _____ Date _____

Task _____

Directions: For each step, write a statement in your own words or draw a picture to help you to select and evaluate methods to complete the task.

1. The outcome of this task:

2. The materials or resources that I need to complete the task:

3. Steps to follow to complete the task:

4. Methods that have worked in the past to complete similar tasks:

5. The method that I will use to complete this task:

6. The steps to follow to use this method:

7. Other methods to try if this method does not work:

8. How I will know that the method(s) I used to complete the task worked:

Guide to Using Organization Strategies

Name _____ Date _____

Items to group _____

Directions: For each step, write a statement in your own words or draw a picture to help you organize or group items.

1. Ways in which these items are similar:

2. Ways in which I will group these items:

3. The names that I will give to these groups:

4. What I will do to remember the items in each group:

5. How I will know that the way I grouped the items will help me to remember them:

Collaborative Model for Study Skills Programs

Inclusive and special educators must work collaboratively to design and implement effective study skills programs in the curriculum.

The continued emphasis on inclusion in education, as well as use of Response to Intervention methodology (see Chapter 1), requires improved collaboration among educators. Full inclusion should provide students with appropriate opportunities to learn and must be collaboratively implemented. This chapter discusses the roles of inclusive and special educators in collaborative efforts to ensure effective implementation of study skills to differentiate instruction for students with diverse and special needs.

Program collaboration involves the continuous exchange of expertise (i.e., knowledge, skills) between special and inclusive educators (Hoover & Patton, 2005). Study skills topics addressed in the previous chapters must be considered by all professionals involved in ensuring an appropriate education for all students. If inclusion is to be effective, students must become proficient in using study skills and study strategies, and professionals must collaborate in designing and implementing effective study skills programs. According to Idol (2002), successful collaboration includes a variety of skills, abilities, and attitudes, such as a desire to learn from others; the ability to communicate in a positive manner, support collaborative efforts, and engage in group problem solving; and a positive attitude toward the collaborative process.

In addition, for collaboration to work effectively, a variety of educators and other significant people must become actively involved in the process to best meet special needs, including study skills needs. Table 7.1, developed from information found in Idol (2002) and Hoover and Patton (2005), identifies key members of a collaborative team and their critical roles in the implementation of a comprehensive study skills program. As shown, collaboration involves support from several people, ranging from the school principal and teachers to parents and other community members. Collectively, these members can provide a comprehensive program within a collaborative model to assist students to acquire, master, apply, and generalize a variety of study skills.

Establishing a Collaborative Study Skills Program

One model that may be followed by special and inclusive educators to ensure effective collaboration in implementing an integrated study skills program is illustrated in Figure 7.1. The model, adapted from Hoover and Patton (2005), reflects the

Table 7.1
Collaboration Team Members and Study Skills Education

Member	Role Significance in Study Skills Education
School principal	Provides support, motivation, and overall leadership
Inclusive educator	Plans, implements, and monitors classroom-based study skills program
Special educator	Develops differentiated study skills strategies and accommodations
School counselor	Provides value-added support beyond the classroom
Paraprofessionals	Provide individualized study skills instructional support
Parents	Provide home-based support of classroom study skills program
Community	Offers community resources and programs to assist study skills programs

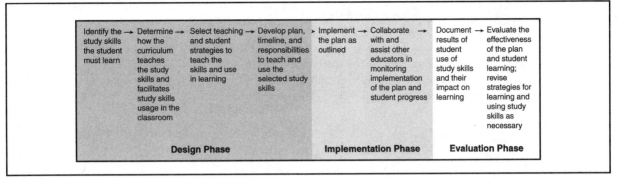

Figure 7.1. Collaborative model for teaching study skills. Adapted from *Curriculum Adaptations for Students with Learning and Behavior Problems: Differentiating Instruction To Meet Diverse Needs* (3rd ed.), by J. J. Hoover and J. R. Patton, 2005, Austin, TX: PRO-ED. Copyright 2005 by PRO-ED, Inc. Adapted with permission.

primary goal of ensuring consistent implementation of a study skills program across class settings. This collaborative study skills model includes three phases—design, implementation, and evaluation—and may be applied easily when establishing a Response to Instruction program relative to teaching study skills.

Design Phase

Study skills used frequently and regularly in one education classroom may also be implemented effectively in other classes. During the design phase, educators identify specific study skills students must use to successfully learn in special and/or inclusive classrooms. Once identified, the curriculum is analyzed to determine specific content, instructional strategies and settings, and management procedures used to facilitate study skills development.

Through various assessment procedures and instruments, including the Study Skills Inventory (Form 4.1) and the guides for identifying study skill needs discussed in Chapter 5, teachers select appropriate study skills that students must acquire and use. Once the study skills that require immediate teaching have been selected, teachers should complete a plan for implementing those study skills in inclusive and/or special education classrooms. The Guide for Program Implementation of Study Skills (Form 7.1) is used for documenting and outlining a program for teaching study skills to ensure that they are implemented consistently in both inclusive and special class settings. The form also serves as a reference for program evaluation of study skills usage in response to an intervention program. This guide may be used to document program implementation in both inclusive and special education settings.

The plan outlines several important factors related to the effective implementation of study skills. Additionally, the information documented in the Study Skills Inventory (Form 4.1) is used to help complete Form 7.1. The study skills that require teaching are documented, along with a specific objective that pertains to each study skill. After outlining the study skills objective, teachers document specific teaching strategies to achieve this objective. Form 7.1 also provides an opportunity to delineate how the study skills program will be implemented, its duration, and the basis for evaluating the plan and objective. This information serves as important feedback to educators as educational progress, including response to study skills instruction, is evaluated for students with special needs.

Implementation Phase

Once the plan for teaching the study skills has been developed (Form 7.1), it is implemented by the inclusive education teacher with support from the special educator. For effective program collaboration to exist, the special educator should assist the inclusive education teacher with program implementation by providing support necessary to achieve the study skills program objectives. The special educator should also assist with the monitoring and documenting of student progress.

If a study skills program is to succeed, both inclusive and special educators must be involved in the process. To assist inclusive and special educators in the overall collaborative process, guidelines are provided on Forms 7.2 and 7.3. The first set of guidelines is from the perspective of the inclusive education teacher, and the second set is from that of the special educator. These guidelines, adapted from Hoover and Patton (2005), reflect the overall purpose of collaboration in implementing study skills instruction to meet diverse needs in a variety of educational settings. These guidelines emphasize flexibility in teaching and represent a commitment to using different study skills until all students in the class receive an appropriate education.

The major area of emphasis for special educators is to provide *support* to educators in inclusive classrooms. This includes assisting in developing or gathering materials, devising study skills ideas, and differentiating curriculum to effectively teach study skills to special learners. Collaborative efforts adhering to these guidelines help to ensure effective study skills usage to meet diverse needs in the classroom.

Evaluation Phase

It is critical to evaluate students' study skills usage, especially as a component of Response to Intervention. Teachers should monitor the effects of the study skills used by discussing them with students on a regular basis. A simple self-monitoring checklist, based on information gathered through the Study Skills Inventory (Form 4.1), could easily be developed and completed daily by the student to record study skills usage. When the plan suggests study techniques that involve readily observable behaviors, the teacher might also complete the simple checklist indicating the frequency of the observed study skills used by the student. This ongoing monitoring of the program will provide summative evaluative data of the effects on the desired study skills goal (e.g., improved weekly test scores, increased attention during writing class, number of completed assignments).

In addition to evaluating the effects of specific student uses of study skills, educators should evaluate the overall study skills program. This may be accomplished through periodic discussions about the program to identify and resolve potential problems that arise. Although minor program changes may be indicated, major changes should not occur, unless necessary, until the program has been implemented for the specified amount of time (e.g., 5 weeks, 10 weeks). Careful and cooperative planning during the development stage reduces the need for making significant and major program changes. Upon completion of the study skills program, all educators involved should review the evaluative information and determine the program's effects on the desired study skills objectives. Decisions concerning subsequent changes are then made, and continued monitoring and documenting of effectiveness occur.

As emphasized, the interaction between inclusive and special educators is critically important. Well-formulated plans will fail if educators are not sensitive to each other's needs. Interpersonal relationship skills are crucial to the development, implementation, and evaluation stages of a study skills program. Interpersonal characteristics relate directly to the success or failure of study skills instruction for students with learning problems in inclusive settings. The collaborative skills that educators use to interact with each other are equally as important as the study skills information shared during the development, implementation, and evaluation process.

Collaborative Skills for Effective Change

A significant challenge confronting special and inclusive education teachers is that of working effectively with other educators to ensure appropriate education in inclusive settings. As expectations associated with full inclusion, the No Child Left Behind Act of 2001 (NCLB), Response to Intervention, and standards-based education continue, the need for collaboration in instruction also increases (Hoover & Patton, 2005). For example, according to Vaughn, Linan-Thompson, and Hickman (2003), as the Response to Intervention movement becomes a major methodology for determining need for special services, a paradigm shift must also occur. In addition, NCLB requires that all students, including those with special needs, be educated and assessed within state curricula. These and similar mandates require standards to be aligned, instruction to be differentiated, and efforts to be collaborated to successfully meet diverse educational needs. Therefore, to support these ongoing reform efforts, educators need to engage in productive change, which includes placing greater emphasis on student uses of study skills and study strategies in the classroom.

Facilitating the Process of Change

The use of study skills to differentiate and improve instruction in inclusive settings requires that teachers make one or more changes within the classroom setting. Teachers may change, for example, seating arrangements, assignments, study strategies, groupings, reward structures, or classroom rules. For change to be successful, according to Weiner (2003), simultaneous reforms in professional development, curriculum, and collaboration must also occur. Knowledge of (a) the general process for creating and implementing change and (b) the major aspects of curricular change help to make the implementation of a study skills program more successful.

The process for effective change includes four major elements (Hoover & Patton, 2005). Change best occurs when the following change elements exist:

1. awareness of the change possibility;
2. interest in change;
3. time to consider the potential worth of the proposed change; and
4. execution of the proposed change on a small, specific scale prior to full implementation.

Prior to making changes, educators must consider the need for and the feasibility of implementing study skills changes in their classrooms. Once the need is determined, teachers must be interested in creating change by differentiating instruction to include greater and more widespread use of study skills by students. If teachers show little interest in and commitment to supporting uses of study skills, they will not make an effort to change the study skills and study strategies usage in the classroom. Proponents of change must work to show other teachers the value of change associated with study skills. Once the teachers see the value of change, the educators should outline a program that specifies study skills to be addressed, by following procedures such as those outlined in Figure 7.1.

Once the plan has been developed and specific study skills outlined, time must be provided to teachers to consider the value of the proposed study skills changes prior to implementation. Final adjustments and revisions should be made, and then the implementation and monitoring of the study skills program changes should begin. Adhering to Hoover and Patton's (2005) change elements facilitates successful development and usage of study skills in inclusive classrooms.

Hoover (2001) discussed several teaching aspects inherent to successful instructional change. They include ensuring that educators recognize that

1. Change impacts individuals and is a process, not a single event.
2. Change requires learning a new skill or developing new meanings or appreciation of existing skills or knowledge.
3. Change is perceived in different ways depending on experiences, roles, or job tasks.
4. Many events, not always in the control of teachers, may influence the actual implementation of change.
5. Change can be facilitated effectively following an organized process.
6. Developing a capacity to change is one ultimate goal so future changes become easier.

The amount of time required to progress through the change elements and address these teaching aspects varies. The model for program collaboration (see Figure 7.1) necessitates that these change elements and aspects be addressed initially in the development stage and emphasized continually throughout the implementation and evaluation stages. The Checklist for Effective Change in Teaching Study Skills (Form 7.4) can be used to evaluate whether the change elements and related teaching aspects discussed above are present. The checklist may be used as a guide to ensure that meaningful changes occur as study skills program aspects are revised and taught. If change in the study skills program is required, adherence to these principles, along with the information discussed previously, may assist in successful planning and implementation. Each of the critical factors listed in Form 7.4 contributes to successful change, with the primary theme being one of cooperative planning within a problem-solving and collaborative structure.

Requisite Communication Skills

Positive communication skills are necessary for educators to create and implement effective change to make study skills education successful. Hoover and Patton (2005) recommend the following communication skills that help to build and maintain professional working relationships:

- Knowing one's own needs and limits of ability
- Clarifying one's own expectations
- Conveying respect, empathy, and understanding toward others
- Establishing and maintaining positive rapport
- Becoming effective, careful, and interested listeners
- Avoiding the selection and implementation of solutions until all or most relevant information has been gathered

- Supporting others' efforts and needs relative to change
- Being nonjudgmental and tolerant toward others
- Becoming informed and knowledgeable about the topics and issues related to program collaboration
- Introducing knowledge and skills to others gradually and systematically in an objective and nonthreatening manner

Special and inclusive educators should consider these communication skills as they undertake collaborative efforts in the development, implementation, and evaluation of a study skills program to differentiate instruction to meet diverse needs.

Guide for Program Implementation of Study Skills

Student Name _____

Completed by _____ Date _____

Study Skills Needed (Check all that apply)

☐ Reading rate	☐ Library usage	☐ Notetaking and outlining	☐ Time management
☐ Listening	☐ Reference materials	☐ Report writing	☐ Self-management
☐ Graphic aids	☐ Test taking	☐ Oral presentations	☐ Organization

Study skills currently taught in the curriculum _____

Implementation plan

Objectives _____

Timeline _____

Resources _____

Teaching strategies _____

Evaluation data to record _____

Assessment procedures to document or record evaluation data _____

_____

Role of inclusive educator _____

Role of special educator _____

Support needed to implement plan _____

_____

Summary of evaluation data _____

_____

_____

Summary of student's response to study skills instruction _____

_____

_____

Collaboration Guidelines for the Inclusive Education Teacher

Directions: Check each item completed in the implementation of a study skills program.

Effective implementation of a study skills program occurs when the inclusive educator . . .

- ☐ Assists in gathering information related to study skills that require development and usage
- ☐ Facilitates use of the study skills to differentiate instruction on a regular basis for the specified amount of time
- ☐ Documents the effectiveness of the study skills program and student uses of the study skills
- ☐ Teaches flexibly to reduce potential problems resulting from changes that occur as study skills instruction is implemented
- ☐ Explores options for teaching study skills through consultation with other educators, especially special education personnel
- ☐ Initially uses the study skills of immediate relevance and does not attempt to add too many at one time
- ☐ Uses different strategies and techniques to achieve appropriate study skills use by all students
- ☐ Implements instruction in a manner that ensures smooth transitions into the use of different study skills and study strategies
- ☐ Prior to implementation, anticipates and accounts for potential problems that may arise from use of new study skills by students
- ☐ Uses study skills and study strategies that are most compatible with existing classroom structures, routines, and student styles of learning

Summary of study skills program efforts: _____

_____

_____

_____

FORM 7.3

Collaboration Guidelines for the Special Educator

Directions: Check each item completed in the implementation of a study skills program.

Effective implementation of a study skills program occurs when the special educator . . .

☐ Assists in gathering and interpreting information related to study skills that potentially require development

☐ Assists with the adaptations of materials to facilitate use of study skills if necessary (e.g., by simplifying assignment levels)

☐ Collaborates with inclusive educators concerning the appropriate selection and use of study skills

☐ Provides suggestions and materials for simple record keeping about effectiveness of study skills used in the inclusive classroom

☐ Provides direct study skills assistance, when possible and appropriate, to inclusive educators

☐ Supports inclusive educators' efforts to differentiate curriculum to teach study skills to meet diverse needs in the classroom

☐ Provides study skills recommendations to the general education teacher, when possible, within the existing structure of the inclusive classroom to increase student success

☐ Assists inclusive educators in anticipating and accounting for potential problems related to the introduction and use of different study skills and strategies

☐ Provides supplemental educational materials to support study skills instruction in the general education classroom when necessary

☐ Recommends to the inclusive educator relevant study skills similar to those implemented in the special education classroom to ensure consistency in the student's education

Summary of study skills program efforts: _____

_____

_____

_____

Checklist for Effective Change in Teaching Study Skills

Student Name _____

Completed by _____ Date _____

Study skills program area(s) requiring change: _____

_____

Reason for change: _____

_____

Timeline for creating change: _____

_____

Directions: Check item to ensure collaborative efforts exist to create effective change.

☐ Educators perceive change areas as important aspects to address in teaching study skills.

☐ Inclusive and special educators cooperatively establish the direction for changes to the study skills program.

☐ Educators acquire professional growth relative to the study skills issues or tasks being changed.

☐ The number of factors associated with the educational situation and the study skills program (e.g., adaptations, differentiating instruction) is kept to a manageable level (i.e., educators do not attempt to change too much too quickly).

☐ Cooperation among educators is kept open, honest, and positive.

☐ Communication among educators is kept open, honest, and positive.

☐ Change is collaboratively planned by those most directly responsible for implementing the change.

☐ Problem-solving sessions remain on task and specific to the study skills to be taught.

☐ Educators respect the process of change and varying capacities for change (i.e., the fact that different individuals adapt or change more slowly or quickly than others).

☐ Administrative support exists to create and implement the change to the study skills program.

8

Home-Based Study Skills Programs

The support of parents in the overall study skills program provides necessary and interrelated connections among life skills, school, and the home.

Throughout this book the discussion emphasizes the importance of study skills acquisition, maintenance, and generalization for students with learning problems to meet both school and lifelong needs. Critical support for study skills education is also found in home-based practices that parents can implement easily. As illustrated in Figure 8.1, an effective study skills program affects and is affected by the home, life skills, and the school. In addition, the emphasis of student study skills use at home, at school, and as lifelong resources complements and enhances study skills use in each of the three areas, showing the importance of such skills development across one's entire life.

This chapter provides a discussion of home-based support for students with learning problems as they develop and use study skills. The suggestions for home practices are made to help teachers more easily obtain parental support for their school efforts at home.

Home-Based Support

A major goal parents have for their children is that they develop the skills necessary to lead independent and productive lives once formal schooling ends (Hoover, 2004a). Home involvement to support schooling is very important, especially for students with learning and behavior problems (Hoover & Patton, 2005). For students to best succeed in school, parents and teachers need to establish collaborative relationships. Parents want suggestions about how to help their children have an equal opportunity to compete in a climate that emphasizes individual achievement, growth, and personal satisfaction. One way in which parents may have this impact is through support, at home, of study skills development and use. Parents can make a long-lasting contribution to the development of their children's effective study habits by supporting school and classroom programs.

Effective study habits provide a student the best chance to succeed with tasks in school. The inability to study well contributes to lost learning and other educational opportunities. Also, the effective demonstration of acquired knowledge and

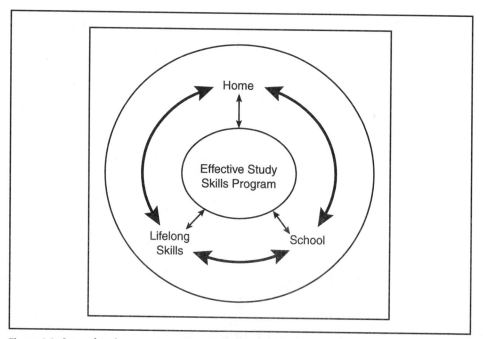

Figure 8.1. Interrelated connections of study skills use.

skills to parents and educators is not possible if one has poor study skills. Good study habits minimize failures in different learning situations as students better understand how to function in different situations as well as how to best learn and demonstrate acquisition of important information. Effective study skills programs in school, along with home support, contribute both to success in school and to developing independent lifelong skills.

The Study Skills Home Inventory (Form 8.1) is an easy-to-use rating scale for parents to document their perceptions about their children's study skills abilities. This quick screening device serves as a place to begin with parents who are interested in developing a study skills program at home. The inventory lists two to five critical elements associated with each main study skill area. After completing this inventory, the parent should meet with the teacher to discuss the results. At the meeting, the teacher may bring any information gathered from a school-based assessment as discussed in Chapter 2. Specific study skills that parents may address at home should be identified, along with strategies for parental support at home. Ongoing monitoring of the home-based program also should occur. The activities and strategies discussed in the remainder of this chapter are examples of the types of tasks parents may attempt at home with their children to further develop study skills and support a classroom-based study skills program, while also developing the children's lifelong skills.

Parental Support in Developing Study Skills

A study skills program should assist students in acquiring and maintaining study skills proficiency throughout their formal schooling and beyond. A home-based program should be developed and followed in ways similar to the school program. Teachers should encourage study skills use at school, and parents can provide valuable support at home. Study skills development at home should include the following types of support:

- Ongoing parent interactions with student efforts in school
- Home reinforcement of study skills acquired and used in school
- Parent understanding of potential school difficulties encountered by students through examination of the study skills used to complete different assignments
- Parent opportunity to assist children in correcting prior study skills errors as they are remediated through practice at home
- Parental encouragement to complete homework or other tasks in a timely and efficient manner

Helping students with study skills at home provides rewarding experiences for both parents and children. A home-based study skills program should include the following types of activities:

- Discuss different study skills with students to help them understand their importance in learning and completing assigned tasks.
- Discuss with students how they approach different learning tasks, and explore their use of different study skills.
- Demonstrate the proper use of necessary study skills during homework or other related tasks.
- Identify a specific time and place for after-school studying at home.

- Discuss completed assignments and tests on a regular basis to help students understand why using different study skills contributed to correct responses.
- Point out and discuss apparent study skills errors from results of completed assignments and tests.
- Emphasize the importance of study skills as a means of assuming responsibility for one's own learning.
- Encourage and help students in the overall planning, organizing, and evaluating of their use of study skills to complete assigned work.

Recommendations for Specific Skills Areas

Continued use of study skills in school and at home allows students to assume responsibility for their own learning and facilitates the ongoing development and use of the study habits. Specific suggestions for parents to help students at home are provided in the following sections for each of the 12 study skills.

Reading Rate

Effective home-based programs emphasize the student's proper use of reading rates. The following activities assist students in developing and strengthening their reading rate abilities. These activities emphasize parental guidance designed to help students identify and use specific reading rates at home.

Home-Based Practices
- Review with children their schoolwork in reading, discussing the different reading rates they used to successfully complete the work.
- Help children to review quickly a book's index or table of contents to find the approximate place where specific answers may be found.
- Ask children different types of questions related to a reading selection. These questions should provide opportunities to use the different reading rates. Discuss the use of the various rates to respond to the questions.
- Discuss with children when they should use each type of reading rate at school and home. Identify similarities between situations at school and home where the same type of reading rate applies.
- As children initially encounter and review different types of reading materials at home (e.g., newspapers, magazines, recipes, assembly instructions, book club materials), discuss why some reading rates are more appropriate to use than others with the various materials.
- Help children to complete homework efficiently by periodically discussing the use of various reading rates for different types of assignments (e.g., studying for a test, reviewing material, answering math word problems, reading a newspaper or magazine).
- Develop with children a chart that highlights general uses of each reading rate and post the chart in the study area of the home. Remind children to refer to this chart prior to beginning homework or other work-related tasks.
- Set aside a time at home (10 to 15 minutes) a couple of days each week for discussing different oral and written tasks completed at school that required reading. Provide children an opportunity to describe the activities, and discuss

with them their use of different reading rates to complete the tasks. Ensure that different subject areas are covered.

- Evaluate and discuss with children the reading rate used to complete a task at home, highlighting the appropriateness or inappropriateness of the specific rate used. Explore alternative reading rates if others are more appropriate for the particular task in question. If applicable, help children to see that they could have started a recreational activity sooner had a more efficient reading rate been used to complete the task.

Listening

Effective home-based programs to develop listening skills should encourage learners to use good listening practices whenever verbal interactions occur. The following activities represent some ways that parents can assist students with developing effective listening skills at home.

Home-Based Practices
- Repeat important items and emphasize key points in verbal interactions.
- Use visual aids to supplement verbal directions, such as those depicting chores or other household responsibilities.
- Provide frequent summaries of oral messages to children if they have difficulty remembering such instructions.
- Provide children the opportunity to respond to oral messages once they have been stated.
- Discuss with children how they attend to listening tasks in school.
- Develop and post "good listener" rules and periodically review them at home.
- After reading a story aloud to children, discuss with them the contents of what they heard and what it means.
- Encourage children to relate what they hear to their own experiences and knowledge by spending a few minutes each day reflecting on oral messages.

Graphic Aids

When assisting learners at home with the development of graphic aids skills, it is essential to emphasize that such aids often comprise an integral and necessary part of written or oral presentations. This may be accomplished with parental support and guidance, as suggested in the following activities.

Home-Based Practices
- Spend a few minutes each week viewing and interpreting graphic aids with children.
- When planning family trips or outings, allow children to refer to maps or other visuals.
- Ensure that learners study graphic directions when assembling items at home.
- Ask children on a regular basis to discuss one graphic aid used in school, explaining why it was useful in the context in which it appeared.
- Develop with learners graphic illustrations depicting daily household responsibilities (e.g., cleaning room, putting clothes in drawers).

- Find examples of different graphs (e.g., picture, circle, pie, bar, line) and review with children the meanings associated with each.
- When reviewing schoolwork or reading with children, ask some questions that require accurate interpretation of visual materials.
- Provide ongoing support for children's use of graphic aids, continually emphasizing their importance to written and oral forms of reporting information.

Library Usage

The development of library skills at home provides necessary support to students whether or not they are required to use the library on a regular basis at school. Knowledge gained from parents' efforts to assist with the development of library usage skills is something students may use throughout their lives.

Home-Based Practices
- Help learners to develop samples of catalog cards or computer printouts and compare them with the actual catalog system in the library.
- Allow learners to develop their own library of books at home.
- Attend library activities with children on a regular basis.
- Use library facilities to help children develop and expand interests in different topics.
- Discuss with children the purposes of different types of library assignments in school.
- Make a list with children of the steps to follow to find a book in the school library and place the list in one of their daily notebooks.
- Periodically review the steps for locating material in the library along with the purposes for using a library.
- Encourage children to consult reference materials at home as the need arises.
- Ask children to explain the catalog system used in their school library and help them to develop a similar system for use in their home library of materials.

Reference Materials

Home-based programs should involve guided direction to students as they attempt to identify, locate, and use reference materials to complete both school requirements and recreational tasks. Various practices at home may facilitate the development of the reference materials study skills through cooperative efforts between parents and their children.

Home-Based Practices
- Develop with children a system for recording information and ensure that they follow that system each time they use reference materials.
- At the beginning of each week, help children to identify appropriate reference materials needed for projects that must be completed during that week.
- Discuss with children different types of topics, asking them to identify appropriate sources to gather information about the topics.
- Develop with children a list of different reference materials and include one or two sentences that describe each material. Post this in the study area in the home.

- Provide learners with practice in locating information through the use of guide words. Present a guide word and a source for locating information through use of that guide word.

- Help children critique their completed note cards to ensure that all important information was correctly documented from the reference materials. Discuss what could be done to ensure inclusion of omitted material in the future.

- Upon completion of a project in which reference materials were used, review how and in what ways the materials were used and for which purposes. Be certain to discuss strengths and weaknesses related to the efficient and effective use of the reference materials.

Test Taking

The home-based program for assisting with development of test-taking skills should be ongoing and involve parent–child discussions about preparing and studying for tests, taking tests, reviewing completed tests, and correcting test-taking errors.

Home-Based Practices
- Review studying procedures as children prepare for a test.

- Help children generate possible questions related to the test topics.

- Develop test questions and have children complete them in practice sessions, ensuring that they use good test-taking skills. Review with them their test-taking skills on completion.

- Develop with children different types of test questions (e.g., essay, multiple choice, true/false, short-answer, matching) to help them learn skills for answering each type of question.

- Review completed tests with children, exploring test-taking errors.

- Periodically discuss and review with children the importance and purposes of completing tests.

- Develop with children a list of good test-taking skills and post it in the study area at home.

- Time children as they complete practice test items to help them determine how long they need to complete various items.

- Review with children different types of directions found in tests, ensuring that they understand the terminology (e.g., compare, match, list, evaluate, contrast, select, discuss, critique).

- Discuss with children the options available for improving test-studying, test-taking, and test-reviewing errors.

Notetaking and Outlining

Home-based programs to improve notetaking and outlining skills are usually related to school assignments and tasks. Therefore, parents must be aware of when and in what class periods students usually take notes or complete outlines so they can reinforce appropriate skills at home. This knowledge is important in parent–child discussions about taking notes, completing outlines, and using these notes and outlines for future reference.

Home-Based Practices

- Spend a few minutes each evening reviewing class notes completed that day in school.

- Provide practice sessions for taking notes or generating outlines from material read in magazines or newspapers.

- Develop a format with children for taking notes during different class periods and review this format with them on a regular basis.

- Read a short story or passage with children and help them develop an outline highlighting main and supporting ideas.

- Help children to develop simple abbreviations for frequently used words or phrases and review them on a regular basis. Also, check to see that the children use these abbreviations when taking notes at school.

- Discuss with and show children the direct connection between good notes and other related activities, such as studying for tests, writing reports, and preparing for the next day's activities.

- Provide children with an outline of a topic in which only main headings are provided. Instruct them to add one or two subheadings for each main heading.

- Encourage children to develop outlines or notes whenever it may assist them in completing tasks at home.

Report Writing

Effective home-based programs for developing the study skill of report writing should supplement the skills and tasks that students engage in at school. Written reports completed at home have a greater chance of being completed effectively if parents assist with this important task. A variety of practices may be used at home to assist students in their development of report-writing abilities.

Home-Based Practices

- Provide periodic review of children's completed written reports and discuss with them how they went about completing their papers.

- Monitor the development of written reports during the major stages of the process.

- Assist learners in proofreading their written work.

- Encourage children to research and write brief reports about topics of interest that arise during activities or discussions at home.

- Provide opportunities for children to obtain experiences related to topics they are writing about in school (e.g., trips to museums, the zoo, community places).

- Keep a family log or newspaper of events and encourage all to contribute, using proper report-writing skills.

- Provide ongoing support of children's report-writing efforts and products through positive praise and constructive feedback, and encourage children to continue with these writing efforts.

Oral Presentations

A home-based program for developing oral presentation skills emphasizes their importance while simultaneously providing a safe and caring environment for students to practice these skills. Various practices may be effective at home as parents and learners work cooperatively on this area.

Home-Based Practices

- Discuss the purpose of each oral presentation with children to ensure that they understand what the presentation should accomplish.
- Structure the situation at home so that learners may practice delivering the presentation in different ways (e.g., standing, seated).
- Develop with children steps to follow to prepare for the oral presentation and monitor progress as steps are completed.
- Develop a weekly family time when members orally present or discuss something of interest to them, encouraging proper oral presentation skills.
- Provide time and a place at home where children may practice the delivery in private.
- Develop with children an outline or script of the oral presentation, making certain that approximately half of the actual presentation is documented and is available for referral during the practices or actual presentation.
- Help children to identify the appropriate number of times they need to rehearse a presentation prior to delivery. Ensure that rehearsals are completed over the course of several days prior to the formal presentation at school.

Time Management

A home-based program for developing the study skill of time management should facilitate students' effective use of time at home and at school. It should be structured in ways that allow learners freedom to develop their own time schedules, execute those schedules, review the results, and adjust schedules accordingly. A variety of practices exist to assist in the development of effective time management.

Home-Based Practices

- Develop semester and monthly schedules with learners, showing deadlines for various activities and personal goals. Post this in the study area in the home.
- Develop time schedules for home activities in which different family members have tasks to complete.
- Review weekly schedules with children at the end of each week, reflecting on the accuracy of their time projections for the week.
- Periodically review daily schedules with children, helping them to see the strengths and weaknesses in their schedules.
- Develop after-school schedules with learners that include homework time, family time, or time for recreational activities. Review efforts to maintain the developed schedules.
- Encourage children to discuss their time management procedures, focusing on how their approaches have worked for them.
- Have children complete a weekly time schedule at the beginning of the week, and then document actual time spent on various activities during the week. Compare actual time spent with projected time for the activities.
- Encourage children to begin each new daily or weekly schedule with positive thoughts about maintaining the schedule, without dwelling on previous time management errors.

- Encourage children to keep a log of how much time they spend on selected activities over a specified period of time. Periodically review the log to determine if too much or too little time is being spent on each activity and adjust time allotments accordingly.

- Assist learners, through ongoing discussions, with the development, monitoring, and implementation of various time management schedules pertaining to school, home, and personal tasks and goals.

Self-Management

The use of self-management or self-control techniques at home may promote consistency between strategies implemented at school and completion of schoolwork at home. Parents can easily support a self-management program at home, provided they understand the program and how it may benefit their child at home.

Home-Based Practices
- Discuss with children their behavioral expectations at school and at home, emphasizing similarities between the two locations.

- Review children's self-management charts with them on a regular basis, providing positive support for their efforts.

- Post in the children's study area at home a list of steps to follow to implement a simple self-management program.

- Identify with the learner one or two behaviors to maintain or improve at home. Jointly develop all recording sheets and monitor behaviors for a specified period of time.

- Assist children in evaluating their progress through discussions of self-management and have them describe the effectiveness of one self-management program at school and at home.

- Once specific target behaviors have been identified for a self-management program, consistently implement the behavioral expectations at home.

Organization

The use of organizational skills at home to complete homework or otherwise support classroom learning is essential for students with learning problems to succeed. Parents may easily support effective management of learning at home. Educators may also acquire a greater understanding of a student's organizational strengths and weaknesses by becoming familiar with how students organize their learning at home.

Home-Based Practices
- Review children's organizational strategies used at school to maintain consistency between home and school.

- Help children to manage their learning time at home by developing a checklist of steps to follow to organize home learning and post it in the home study area.

- Support children in their own efforts to organize their own home learning.

- Review weekly assignment and test schedules with children, and help them to plan how and where they will complete the tasks and study for tests.
- Discuss the importance of effective organizational skills in academic achievement.
- Assist children to adjust the organization of their tasks to meet unexpected demands on their time.

FORM 8.1

Study Skills Home Inventory

Student Name _____

Completed by _____ Date _____

Directions: Based on your observations and interactions with your child at home, rate your child's usage of each of the following subskills. Use the following scale: 1 = *not mastered (infrequent use of skill)*; 2 = *partially mastered (needs some improvement)*; 3 = *mastered (regular and appropriate use of skill)*.

Study Skill	Subskills	Rating
Reading rate	1. Uses fast-paced reading rates (skimming, scanning, rapid reading) 2. Uses normal, careful, or study-type reading rates	_____ _____
Listening	1. Attends to listening tasks 2. Applies meaning to verbal messages	_____ _____
Graphic aids	1. Understands purposes of visual material 2. Develops own graphic aids 3. Attends to relevant elements in graphic aids	_____ _____ _____
Library usage	1. Understands and uses catalog system 2. Is able to locate library materials	_____ _____
Reference materials	1. Knows purposes of different reference materials 2. Uses reference materials when necessary	_____ _____
Test taking	1. Organizes written answers or responses 2. Reads and understands directions 3. Identifies test-taking errors 4. Corrects previous test-taking errors 5. Identifies and uses clue words	_____ _____ _____ _____ _____
Notetaking and outlining	1. Uses headings appropriately 2. Records important information 3. Takes well-organized notes 4. Takes clear and concise notes	_____ _____ _____ _____
Report writing	1. Organizes thoughts 2. Uses proper punctuation 3. Uses correct grammar	_____ _____ _____
Oral presentations	1. Freely participates in oral activities 2. Speaks clearly	_____ _____
Time management	1. Organizes daily and weekly activities 2. Prioritizes activities 3. Completes tasks on time 4. Reorganizes time as necessary	_____ _____ _____ _____
Self-management	1. Monitors own behavior 2. Is responsible for own behavior 3. Changes own behavior as necessary	_____ _____ _____
Organization	1. Maintains an organized work area 2. Assembles books and other materials needed for school in an orderly way 3. Manages multiple tasks or assignments 4. Prioritizes the order for successful task completion	_____ _____ _____ _____

Summary comments: _____

_____

_____

References

Baca, L., & Cervantes, H. (2004). *The bilingual special education interface* (4th ed.). Columbus, OH: Merrill.

Bender, W. N. (2002). *Differentiating instruction for students with learning disabilities.* Thousand Oaks, CA: Corwin Press.

Bloom, B. S., Englehart, M. D., Furst, G. J., Hill, W. H., & Krathwohl, D. R. (1956). *Taxonomy of educational objectives: Handbook 1. The cognitive domain.* New York: McKay.

Bos, C., & Vaughn, S. (2006). *Strategies for teaching students with learning and behavior problems.* Boston: Allyn & Bacon.

Brown, L. (2004). Evaluating and managing classroom behavior. In D. D. Hammill & N. R. Bartel (Eds.), *Teaching students with learning and behavior problems* (7th ed., pp. 291–345). Austin, TX: PRO-ED.

Cohen, L., & Spenciner, L. J. (2005). *Teaching students with mild and moderate disabilities: Research-based practices.* Columbus, OH: Merrill/Prentice Hall.

Cronin, M. E., Patton, J. R., & Wood, S. J. (2006). *Life skills instruction for all students with special needs: A practical guide for integrating real-life content into the curriculum* (2nd ed.). Austin, TX: PRO-ED.

Cummins, J., & Sayers, D. (1995). *Brave new schools: Challenging cultural illiteracy through global learning networks.* New York: St. Martin's Press.

Czarnecki, E., Rosko, D., & Pine, E. (1998). How to call up notetaking skills. *Teaching Exceptional Children, 30,* 14–19.

Day, V. P., & Elksnin, L. K. (1994). Promoting strategic learning. *Intervention in School and Clinic, 29*(5), 262–270.

de la Paz, S. (1997). Strategy instruction in planning: Teaching students with learning and writing disabilities to compose persuasive and expository essays. *Learning Disability Quarterly, 20,* 227–248.

Deshler, D., Ellis, E., & Lenz, K. (1996). *Teaching adolescents with learning disorders: Strategies and methods* (2nd ed.). Denver, CO: Love Publishing.

Donovan, M. S., & Cross, C. T. (Eds.). (2002). *Minority students in special and gifted education.* Washington, DC: National Academy Press.

Education Commission of the States. (2003). *No child left behind issue brief: A guide to standards-based assessment.* Denver, CO: Author.

Fagen, S., Long, N. J., & Stevens, D. (1975). *Teaching children self-control.* Columbus, OH: Merrill/Prentice Hall.

Fuchs, D., & Fuchs, L. S. (1994). Inclusive schools movement and the radicalization of special education reform. *Exceptional Children, 60,* 294–309.

Fuchs, D., Mock, D., Morgan, P. L., & Young, C. (2003). Responsiveness-to-instruction intervention: Definitions, evidence, and implications for the learning disabilities construct. *Learning Disabilities: Research & Practice, 18,* 157–171.

Garcia, E. E. (2001). *Hispanic education in the United States: Raíces y alas.* Lanham, MD: Rowman & Littlefield.

Gartin, B. C., Murdick, N. L., Imbeau, M., & Perner, D. E. (2002). *How to use differentiated instruction with students with developmental disabilities in the general education classroom.* Arlington, VA: Council for Exceptional Children.

Gearheart, B. R., Weishahn, M. W., & Gearheart, C. J. (1996). *The exceptional student in the regular classroom* (5th ed.). Columbus, OH: Merrill.

Goldberg, D., & Zwiebel, J. (2005). *The organized student: Teaching children the skills for success in school and beyond.* New York: Fireside.

Harris, A. J., & Sipay, E. R. (1990). *How to increase reading ability.* New York: Longman.

Hasbrouck, J. (2002). *Washington State Reading Initiative.* Olympia: Washington Department of Education.

Heaton, S., & O'Shea, D. (1995). Using mnemonics to make mnemonics. *Teaching Exceptional Children,* pp. 34–35.

Hoover, J. J. (2001). *Class management* (CD-ROM). Boulder: University of Colorado at Boulder, School of Education, BUENO Center.

Hoover, J. J. (2004a). Study skills. In E. A. Polloway, J. R. Patton, & L. Serna (Eds.), *Strategies for teaching learners with special needs* (7th ed.). Columbus, OH: Merrill/Prentice Hall.

Hoover, J. J. (2004b). Teaching students to use study skills. In D. D. Hammill & N. R. Bartel (Eds.), *Teaching students with learning and behavior problems* (7th ed, pp. 347–380). Austin, TX: PRO-ED.

Hoover, J. J. (2005). Special challenges for special needs. In J. J. Hoover (Ed.), *Current issues in special education: Meeting diverse needs in the twenty-first century*. Boulder: University of Colorado, School of Education, BUENO Center.

Hoover, J. J., & Collier, C. (1992). Sociocultural considerations in teaching study strategies. *Intervention in School and Clinic, 27,* 228–232.

Hoover, J. J., & Collier, C. (2003). *Learning styles* (CD-ROM). Boulder: University of Colorado at Boulder, School of Education, BUENO Center.

Hoover, J. J., & Patton, J. R. (2004). Perspective: Differentiating standards-based education for students with diverse needs. *Remedial and Special Education, 25*(2), 74–78.

Hoover, J. J., & Patton, J. R. (2005). *Curriculum adaptations for students with learning and behavior problems: Differentiating instruction to meet diverse needs* (3rd ed.). Austin, TX: PRO-ED.

Hoover, J. J., & Rabideau, D. K. (1995). Semantic webs and study skills. *Intervention in School and Clinic, 30,* 292–296.

Hoover, J. J., & Trujillo-Hinsch, J. (1999). *Test-taking skills of English language learners*. Boulder: University of Colorado, School of Education, BUENO Center.

Idol, L. (2002). *Creating collaborative and inclusive schools*. Austin, TX: PRO-ED.

Individuals with Disabilities Education Improvement Act of 2004, 42 U.S.C. § 12101 *et seq.*

Johnson, D., & Johnson, R. (1998). *Learning together and alone: Cooperative, competitive, and individualistic learning* (5th ed.). Englewood Cliffs, NJ: Prentice Hall.

Kagan, S. (1997). *Cooperative learning*. San Capistrano, CA: Kagan.

Lewis, R. B., & Doorlag, D. H. (2002). *Teaching special students in general education classrooms* (6th ed.). Columbus, OH: Merrill/Prentice Hall.

Linn, L. R., & Herman, J. L. (1997). *A policymaker's guide to standards-led assessment*. Denver, CO: Education Commission of the States.

Maccini, P., & Gagnon, J. C. (2002). Perceptions and applications of NCTM standards by special and general education teachers. *Exceptional Children, 68,* 325–344.

Marks, J. W., Laeys, J. V., Bender, W. N., & Scott, K. S. (1996). Teachers creating learning strategies: Guidelines for classroom creation. *Teaching Exceptional Children, 28*(4), 34–38.

Mastropieri, M. A., & Scruggs, T. E. (1998). Enhancing school success with mnemonic strategies. *Intervention in School and Clinic, 33*(4), 201–208.

McLaughlin, J. A., & Lewis, R. B. (2000). *Assessing special students: Strategies and procedures*. Columbus, OH: Merrill/Prentice Hall.

McLaughlin, W. W., & Shepard, L. A. (1995). *Improving education through standards-based reform*. Stanford, CA: National Academy of Education.

Mercer, C. D., & Mercer, A. R. (2000). *Teaching students with learning problems*. Columbus, OH: Merrill/Prentice Hall.

Morgenstern, J. (1998). *Organizing from the inside out: The foolproof system for organizing your home, your office, and your life*. New York: Holt.

No Child Left Behind Act of 2001, 20 U.S.C. § 6301 *et seq.*

Ogle, D. (1986). A teaching model that develops active reading of expository text. *The Reading Teacher, 39,* 564-570.

O'Malley, J. M., & Pierce, L. V. (1996). *Authentic assessment for English language learners*. Boston: Addison-Wesley.

Ovando, C. J., Collier, V. P., & Combs, M. C. (2003). *Bilingual and ESL classrooms: Teaching in multicultural contexts*. Boston: McGraw Hill.

Polloway, E. A., Patton, J. R., & Serna, L. (2004). *Strategies for teaching learners with special needs* (7th ed.). Columbus, OH: Merrill/Prentice Hall.

Quenemoen, R. F., Lehr, C. A., Thurlow, M. L., & Massanaair, C. B. (2001). *Students with disabilities in standards-based assessment and accountability systems: Emerging issues, strategies, and recommendations*. Minneapolis, MN: National Center on Educational Outcomes.

Roy, P. A. (1990). *Cooperative learning: Students learn together*. Richfield, MN: Author.

Salend, S. J. (2000). *Creating inclusive classrooms: Effective and reflective practices* (4th ed.). Columbus, OH: Merrill/Prentice Hall.

Slavin, R. E. (1991). *Cooperative learning and the collaborative school* (pp. 82–89). Alexandria, VA: Association for Supervision and Curriculum Development.

Smith, T. E. C., Polloway, E. A., Patton, J. R., & Dowdy, C. A. (2000). *Teaching students with special needs in inclusive settings* (3rd ed.). Boston: Allyn & Bacon.

Stainback, S., Stainback, W., East, K., & Sapon-Shevin, M. (1995). Inclusion and the development of a positive self-identity by persons with disabilities. In S. Stainback & W. Stainback (Eds.), *Inclusion: A guide for educators* (pp. 361–366). Baltimore: Brookes.

Thompson, S. J. (2004). Choosing and using accommodations on assessments. *CEC Today, 10*(6), 12.

Vaughn, S., & Fuchs, D. (2003). Redefining learning disabilities as inadequate response to instruction: The promise and potential problems. *Learning Disabilities: Research & Practice, 18,* 137–146.

Vaughn, S., Linan-Thompson, S., & Hickman, P. (2003). Response to instruction as a means of identifying students with reading/learning disabilities. *Exceptional Children, 69,* 391–409.

Wallace, G., & Kauffman, J. M. (1990). *Teaching students with learning and behavior problems*. Columbus, OH: Merrill.

Weiner, H. M. (2003). Effective inclusion: Professional development in the context of the classroom. *Teaching Exceptional Children, 35*(6), 12–18.

Yell, M. (2004, February). *Understanding the three-tier model*. Presentation at the Colorado State Directors of Special Education Meeting, Denver, CO.

About the Authors

John J. Hoover has over 30 years of experience in teaching and research related to the education of students with learning and behavior problems at the elementary, secondary, and postsecondary levels. He has written or cowritten over 50 published articles, textbook chapters, and books, many of which address the topic of accommodating the curricular needs of students with learning problems. Dr. Hoover earned his BA from Illinois State University, MA from Northern Arizona University, and PhD from the University of Colorado, Boulder. He is currently an associate director of the BUENO Center in the School of Education at the University of Colorado, Boulder.

James R. Patton is an educational consultant and adjunct associate professor in the Department of Special Education at the University of Texas, Austin. He has experience teaching students with special needs at the elementary, secondary, and postsecondary levels. His research interests include life skills instruction, transition assessment, lifelong learning, instructional practices and accommodations, and select legal issues related to individuals with special needs. Dr. Patton earned his BS from the University of Notre Dame and his MEd and EdD from the University of Virginia.